It's always time for cake...

Indulgent
CAKES

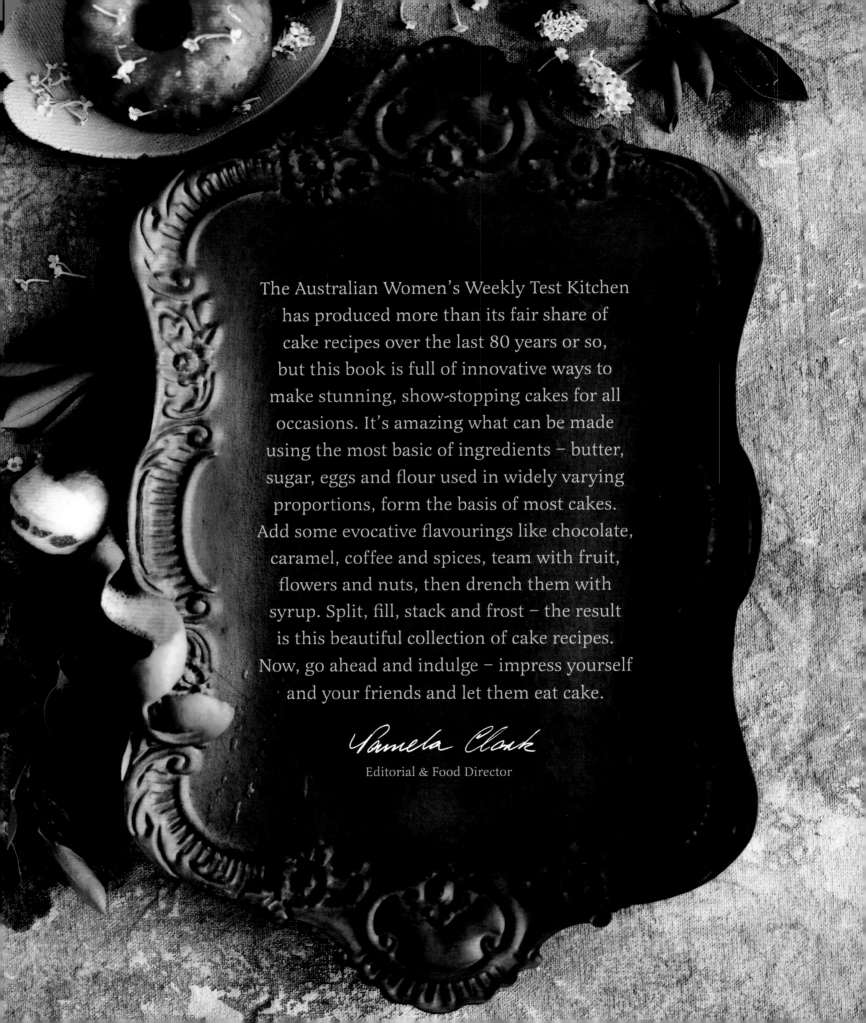

The Australian Women's Weekly Test Kitchen
has produced more than its fair share of
cake recipes over the last 80 years or so,
but this book is full of innovative ways to
make stunning, show-stopping cakes for all
occasions. It's amazing what can be made
using the most basic of ingredients – butter,
sugar, eggs and flour used in widely varying
proportions, form the basis of most cakes.
Add some evocative flavourings like chocolate,
caramel, coffee and spices, team with fruit,
flowers and nuts, then drench them with
syrup. Split, fill, stack and frost – the result
is this beautiful collection of cake recipes.
Now, go ahead and indulge – impress yourself
and your friends and let them eat cake.

Pamela Clark

Editorial & Food Director

Indulgent CAKES

LUSCIOUS CAKES TO DELIGHT YOUR EVERY WHIM

Contents

LUSCIOUS CAKES TO DELIGHT YOUR EVERY WHIM

CHAPTERS

SWEET EXTRAVAGANT CREATIONS TO INSPIRE

INDULGENT CAKES

Chocolate
& COFFEE

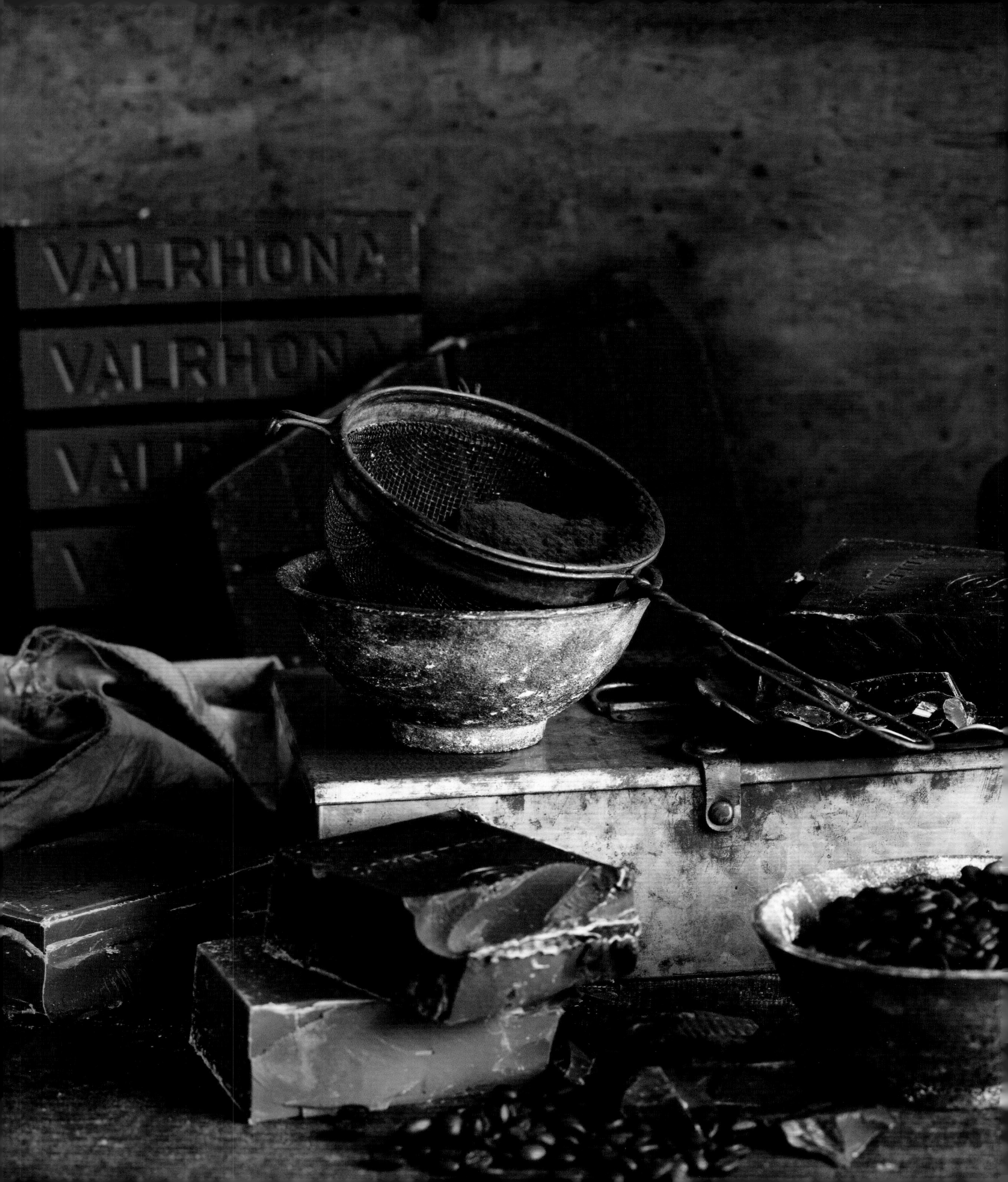
VALRHONA
VALRHONA

THE MAGICAL
PAIRING OF
Chocolate
and coffee
is dark
Seductive
AND INTENSE

Flourless chocolate, PRUNE AND HAZELNUT CAKE

PREP + COOK TIME 1 HOUR 15 MINUTES (+ STANDING) SERVES 10

1 cup (170g) pitted prunes, chopped finely
1/2 cup (125ml) hazelnut-flavoured liqueur
200g (6 1/2 ounces) dark (semi-sweet) chocolate,
 chopped coarsely
125g (4 ounces) butter, softened
5 eggs, separated
2/3 cup (150g) firmly packed brown sugar
1 1/4 cups (180g) ground hazelnuts
2 teaspoons dutch-processed cocoa

HAZELNUT CREAM
300ml pouring cream
2 tablespoons icing (confectioners') sugar
2 tablespoons hazelnut-flavoured liqueur

1 Place prunes and liqueur in a small saucepan; bring to the boil.
Reduce heat; simmer, uncovered, for 2 minutes or until liqueur
is reduced by half. Remove from heat; cool.
2 Meanwhile, preheat oven to 180°C/350°F. Grease a deep 22cm
(9-inch) round cake pan; line base and side with baking paper.
3 Stir chocolate and butter in a small saucepan over low heat
until melted and smooth. Cool to room temperature.

4 Beat egg yolks and sugar in a small bowl with an electric
mixer until thick and creamy. Transfer mixture to a large bowl;
fold in prune mixture, chocolate mixture and ground hazelnuts.
5 Beat egg whites in a small bowl with an electric mixer until
soft peaks form; fold into chocolate mixture, in two batches.
Pour mixture into pan.
6 Bake cake for 50 minutes or until a skewer inserted into the
centre comes out with moist crumbs attached. Stand cake in pan
for 15 minutes; turn cake, top-side up, onto a wire rack to cool.
7 Make hazelnut cream.
8 Dust cake with cocoa; serve with hazelnut cream.

HAZELNUT CREAM Beat cream and sugar in a small bowl
with an electric mixer until firm peaks form. Stir in liqueur.

TECHNIQUES Step 2: see *'lining a round cake pan'*, page 276.
DO-AHEAD The cake can be made a day ahead; store in an
airtight container at room temperature. The hazelnut cream
is best made on the day of serving.

FLOURLESS CHOCOLATE *beetroot cake*

PREP + COOK TIME 2 HOURS (+ REFRIGERATION & COOLING) SERVES 12

300g (9½ ounces) beetroot (beets), peeled,
    cut in 3cm (1¼-inch) pieces
350g (11 ounces) dark chocolate (70% cocoa), chopped
185g (6 ounces) butter, chopped
6 eggs
1 teaspoon vanilla extract
1 cup (220g) firmly packed brown sugar
1 cup (100g) ground hazelnuts
1 teaspoon dutch-processed cocoa

CANDIED BEETROOT

1½ cups (330g) caster (superfine) sugar
1 cup (250ml) water
2 small beetroot (beets) (200g), peeled, sliced thinly
1 tablespoon lemon juice

SWEETENED CRÈME FRAÎCHE

1½ cups (360g) crème fraîche
2 tablespoons icing (confectioners') sugar, sifted
1 teaspoon vanilla extract

1 Cook beetroot in a small saucepan of boiling water for
45 minutes or until tender. Drain, reserving 2 tablespoons
of the cooking liquid. Process beetroot and reserved liquid
until smooth. You should have 1 cup beetroot puree.
2 Preheat oven to 160°C/325°F. Grease a 22cm (9-inch)
springform pan; line base and side with baking paper.
3 Stir chocolate and butter in a small saucepan over low
heat until melted and smooth.

4 Whisk eggs, extract, sugar and ground hazelnuts in a large
bowl until combined. Add chocolate mixture and beetroot puree;
whisk to combine. Pour mixture into pan; cover with foil.
5 Bake cake for 1 hour 10 minutes or until cooked around the
edge with a slight wobble in the centre. Lift up edge of foil to
release steam. Refrigerate cake for at least 3 hours or overnight.
6 Make candied beetroot, then sweetened crème fraîche.
7 Place cake on a platter; dust cake edges with cocoa. Spread top
of cake with sweetened crème fraîche. Top with candied beetroot
and drizzle with reserved syrup.

CANDIED BEETROOT Stir sugar and the water in a small
saucepan over medium heat until sugar dissolves. Bring to the
boil. Add beetroot; cook for 20 minutes or until beetroot slices
become slightly translucent and syrup thickens. Using two forks,
transfer beetroot from syrup to a baking-paper-lined oven tray
to cool. Reserve 1 cup of the syrup; stir in juice.

SWEETENED CRÈME FRAÎCHE Whisk ingredients together
in a small bowl until soft peaks form.

TIP Use a mandoline or V-slicer to slice the beetroot into thin
rounds for candying. They are available from kitchen stores
and Asian supermarkets.
DO-AHEAD The cake and candied beetroot can be made a day
ahead. Store separately in airtight containers in the refrigerator.

Mocha meringue stack

PREP + COOK TIME **1 HOUR 45 MINUTES (+ COOLING)** SERVES **12**

1 tablespoon instant coffee granules
1 teaspoon boiling water
8 egg whites
1 teaspoon cream of tartar
2 cups (440g) raw caster (superfine) sugar
1 tablespoon cornflour (cornstarch)
2 teaspoons white vinegar
2 teaspoons icing (confectioners') sugar

CHOCOLATE SAUCE
180g (5¹/₂ ounces) dark (semi-sweet) chocolate, chopped
30g (1 ounce) unsalted butter, chopped
1 cup (250ml) thickened (heavy) cream
¹/₄ cup (40g) icing (confectioners') sugar

COFFEE CREAM
1 tablespoon instant coffee granules
2 teaspoons boiling water
300ml thickened (heavy) cream
¹/₄ cup (40g) icing (confectioners') sugar
2 tablespoons coffee-flavoured liqueur
300ml thick (double) cream

1 Preheat oven to 120°C/250°F. Line three large oven trays with baking paper.
2 Stir coffee and the water in a small bowl until dissolved. Beat egg whites and cream of tartar in a large bowl with an electric mixer until soft peaks form. Gradually add caster sugar, beating until dissolved between additions. Beat in cornflour, vinegar and coffee mixture on low speed until just combined (overbeating at this stage will cause the meringue to deflate).

3 Drop large serving-spoon-sized amounts of meringue mixture (about ¹/₄ cup) onto trays, 5cm (2-inches) apart; you should get about 24 meringues (see page 16). Bake meringues for 1 hour or until dry to touch. Cool in oven with door ajar.
4 Make chocolate sauce, then coffee cream.
5 Spoon a little coffee cream onto a platter, arrange nine of the meringues on top. Spread the base of each remaining meringue with 2 tablespoons of coffee cream, stacking them into a pyramid shape. Drizzle stack with half the chocolate sauce, then dust with icing sugar. Serve stack immediately with coffee cream and the remaining sauce.

CHOCOLATE SAUCE Stir chocolate, butter and cream in a medium saucepan over low heat until just melted. Remove from heat; gradually whisk in sifted icing sugar. Cool to room temperature (about 20 minutes) until thickened.

COFFEE CREAM Stir coffee and the water in a small bowl until dissolved; refrigerate for 5 minutes. Beat thickened cream, icing sugar, liqueur and coffee mixture in a small bowl with an electric mixer until soft peaks form. Add thick cream; beat until soft peaks form.

TIP The meringues could take up to 1¹/₂ hours to cook, depending on the size of the oven. If you don't have enough space or shelves in your oven, make meringues in two batches.
DO-AHEAD The meringues can be made 2 days ahead; store in an airtight container at room temperature. The sauce can be made several hours ahead; reheat until just warm before serving. Assemble meringue stack close to serving.

Mocha meringue stack

[RECIPE PAGE 14]

MAKING THE MERINGUE

Beat cornflour, vinegar and coffee mixture into the meringue on low speed, or alternatively fold in using a large metal spoon. Make sure that you do so gently to prevent deflating the meringue.

SHAPING THE MERINGUE

Using a large metal kitchen or serving spoon, scoop up about 1/4 cup of the meringue mixture. Hold a second large metal spoon the same size upside down over the meringue, drag it over the mound in an arc shape. As you reach the other side, bring the top of the spoon under the scoop of meringue transferring it onto it in the process. Using the first spoon, push the quenelle-shaped meringue onto the tray.

MAKING THE CHOCOLATE SAUCE

It's a good idea to chop the chocolate and butter into similar-sized pieces, and to use a small heavy-based saucepan. Heat the ingredients over low heat until they are just melted and warmed, stirring to combine.

MAKING THE COFFEE CREAM
Take care not to overbeat the mixture when you're beating the two creams together, as it will only take a few seconds for it to thicken to the desired consistency.

ASSEMBLING THE STACK
Use the back of a spoon, metal palette knife or offset spatula to spread a little of the coffee cream on the base of each meringue, taking care as the shell of the meringue is quite fragile. If you do break one, place it on the bottom of the stack where it will be hidden or make sure you drizzle the chocolate sauce over any cracks.

SERVING
Starting from the top, gently prise each meringue away using a fork and spoon – try and avoid applying too much pressure to the meringues or they will crush. Drizzle with chocolate sauce.

Espresso date cake
WITH CHOCOLATE GLAZE

PREP + COOK TIME **1 HOUR 15 MINUTES** SERVES **10**

1¹/₄ cups (200g) finely chopped dried dates
1¹/₂ tablespoons espresso coffee granules
1¹/₄ cups (310ml) water
1 teaspoon bicarbonate of soda (baking soda)
60g (2 ounces) butter
³/₄ cup (165g) caster (superfine) sugar
2 eggs
1 cup (150g) self-raising flour

CHOCOLATE GLAZE
150g (4¹/₂ ounces) dark (semi-sweet) chocolate,
   chopped coarsely
¹/₃ cup (80ml) thickened (heavy) cream
1 tablespoon golden syrup or corn syrup

1 Preheat oven to 180°C/350°F. Grease a deep 20cm (8-inch) round cake pan; line base and side with baking paper.
2 Combine dates, coffee and the water in a small saucepan; bring to the boil. Remove from heat; stir in bicarbonate of soda. Stand for 5 minutes. Blend or process mixture until smooth.
3 Beat butter and sugar in a small bowl with an electric mixer until pale. Beat in eggs, one at a time, until just combined. Fold in sifted flour, then date mixture. Pour mixture into pan.
4 Bake cake for 50 minutes or until a skewer inserted in the centre comes out with moist crumbs attached. Stand cake in pan for 15 minutes before turning, top-side up, onto a wire rack to cool slightly.
5 Make chocolate glaze.
6 Place cake on a platter. Slowly pour glaze on cake, allowing a little to drip down the side.

CHOCOLATE GLAZE Stir ingredients in a small saucepan over low heat until smooth. Transfer glaze to a small heatpoof jug.

TECHNIQUES Step 1: see *'lining a round cake pan'*, page 276.
DO-AHEAD The cake is best made on the day of serving.

Chilli chocolate
ICE-CREAM TORTE

PREP + COOK TIME 1 HOUR 35 MINUTES (+ REFRIGERATION & FREEZING) SERVES 12

You will need to start this recipe the day before serving.

4 egg whites
1 cup (220g) caster (superfine) sugar
200g (6¹/₂ ounces) dark chocolate (70% cocoa),
   grated coarsely
³/₄ teaspoon ground cardamom
300ml thickened (heavy) cream
200g (6¹/₂ ounces) dark chocolate (70% cocoa), extra,
   grated coarsely

CHILLI CHOCOLATE ICE-CREAM
2 cups (500ml) milk
7 egg yolks
1 cup (220g) caster (superfine) sugar
300g (9¹/₂ ounces) dark chocolate (70% cocoa),
   grated coarsely
1 teaspoon chilli powder
2 cups (500ml) thickened (heavy) cream

1 Make chilli chocolate ice-cream.
2 Preheat oven to 160°C/325°F. Lock the base in a 23cm
(9¹/₄-inch) springform pan upside down; grease, then line base
and side with baking paper.
3 Beat egg whites and sugar in a small bowl with an electric
mixer for 8 minutes or until thick and glossy. Fold in combined
chocolate and cardamom. Spread mixture in pan evenly.

4 Bake meringue for 35 minutes or until firm to touch and
golden. Cool in pan. Using the base of a glass, gently push down
the top of the meringue to create a smooth and level surface.
5 Spoon chilli chocolate ice-cream over meringue base; freeze
for 8 hours or overnight.
6 Before serving, remove cake from pan; stand at room
temperature for 10 minutes. Meanwhile, stir cream and extra
chocolate in a small saucepan over low heat until chocolate melts
and sauce is smooth. Serve torte drizzled with warm sauce.

CHILLI CHOCOLATE ICE-CREAM Place milk in a small saucepan;
bring almost to the boil. Meanwhile, whisk yolks and sugar in
a medium heatproof bowl until pale and creamy. Gradually add
the hot milk, whisking continuously to combine. Place bowl
over a small saucepan of simmering water; cook, stirring, for
4 minutes or until mixture thickens enough to coat the back
of a spoon. Strain mixture through a fine sieve. Whisk chocolate
and chilli into mixture until smooth. Refrigerate 30 minutes.
Beat cream in a small bowl with an electric mixer until
soft peaks form; fold into cooled chocolate mixture. Churn
mixture, in batches, in an ice-cream machine according to the
manufacturer's instructions.

TIP Inserting the base of the springform pan upside down
will make it easier to slide the cake from the base.
DO-AHEAD The torte can be made up to 1 week ahead.
The chocolate sauce can be made up to 3 days ahead; gently
reheat before serving.

Five-layer chocolate espresso cake
[RECIPE PAGES 24 & 25]

Five-layer chocolate
ESPRESSO CAKE

PREP + COOK TIME 2 HOURS (+ COOLING & REFRIGERATION) SERVES 12

You will need to start this recipe the day before. The cake can be made a couple of days ahead, or if you prefer you can make it in stages over 2 days.

DARK CHOCOLATE FUDGE CAKE

50g (1½ ounces) butter, chopped
100g (3 ounces) dark chocolate (70% cocoa), chopped
½ cup (110g) firmly packed brown sugar
1 egg
½ cup (75g) plain (all-purpose) flour
¼ cup (60g) sour cream

WHITE CHOCOLATE CHEESECAKE

¼ cup (60ml) thickened (heavy) cream
125g (4 ounces) white chocolate, chopped
250g (8 ounces) cream cheese, softened
⅓ cup (75g) caster (superfine) sugar
1 egg

ESPRESSO JELLY

3 teaspoons powdered gelatine
1½ cups (375ml) water
2 tablespoons caster (superfine) sugar
1 tablespoon espresso coffee granules

MILK CHOCOLATE MOUSSE

150g (4½ ounces) milk chocolate, chopped
¾ cup (180ml) thickened (heavy) cream

DARK CHOCOLATE GLAZE

200g (6½ ounces) dark chocolate (70% cocoa), chopped
1 tablespoon vegetable oil

CHOCOLATE WAVES

100g (3 ounces) dark chocolate (70% cocoa), chopped finely
1 teaspoon dutch-processed cocoa

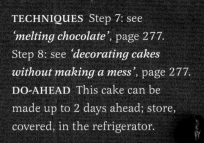

TECHNIQUES Step 7: see *'melting chocolate'*, page 277. Step 8: see *'decorating cakes without making a mess'*, page 277.
DO-AHEAD This cake can be made up to 2 days ahead; store, covered, in the refrigerator.

1 Preheat oven to 160°C/325°F. Unlock the base from a deep 22cm (9-inch) springform pan; invert base, then cover with a piece of baking paper. Lock the ring around the base, over the paper (the paper will extend outside the pan making it easier to remove the cake later). Grease pan; line side with baking paper, extending the paper 5cm (2 inches) above the side.
2 To make dark chocolate fudge cake, stir butter and chocolate in a small saucepan over low heat until smooth. Remove from heat; stir in sugar, then egg, flour and sour cream. Spread mixture into pan; stand until required.
3 To make white chocolate cheesecake, stir cream and chocolate in a small saucepan over low heat until smooth; cool. Beat cream cheese and sugar in a small bowl with an electric mixer until smooth. Beat in cooled chocolate mixture, then egg (do not overbeat). Pour cheesecake mixture over fudge cake in pan. Bake for 30 minutes or until centre of cheesecake is set and has a slight wobble. Cool in oven with door ajar. Refrigerate.
4 To make espresso jelly, sprinkle gelatine over ¼ cup (60ml) of the water in a small heatproof jug. Stand jug in a small saucepan of simmering water, stir until gelatine dissolves; cool. Place the remaining water in a small saucepan with sugar and coffee granules; stir over low heat until sugar and coffee dissolve. Stir in gelatine mixture. Transfer mixture to a medium jug. Refrigerate 30 minutes or until mixture thickens slightly to the consistency of custard. Pour jelly mixture over cheesecake in pan; carefully smooth surface. Refrigerate 30 minutes or until set.

5 To make milk chocolate mousse, stir chocolate in a small heatproof bowl over a small saucepan of simmering water (don't let water touch base of bowl) until smooth; cool. Beat cream in a small bowl with an electric mixer until soft peaks form; fold in cooled chocolate. Spread mousse mixture over jelly in pan; smooth surface. Refrigerate 3 hours or overnight until set.
6 To make dark chocolate glaze, stir chocolate and oil in a small heatproof bowl over a small saucepan of simmering water (don't let water touch base of bowl) until smooth. Cool slightly.
7 Meanwhile, to make chocolate waves, melt half the chocolate (see TECHNIQUES). Remove bowl from pan; stir in remaining chocolate until melted. Spread chocolate thinly over a piece of baking paper. Place a rolling pin under paper; set at room temperature. Break into shards.
8 Remove cake from pan; place on a plate (see TECHNIQUES). Working quickly, spread glaze over top and side of cake. Refrigerate for 10 minutes or until glaze is set. Decorate cake with chocolate waves; dust with cocoa.

[PHOTOGRAPH PAGES 22 & 23]

Chocolate orange mousse cake
[RECIPE PAGES 28 & 29]

CHOCOLATE ORANGE
mousse cake

PREP + COOK TIME 50 MINUTES (+ STANDING & REFRIGERATION) SERVES 12

You will need to start this recipe the day before.

200g (6 ounces) dark chocolate (70% cocoa), chopped
20g (³/₄ ounce) butter
6 eggs, separated
¹/₂ cup (110g) caster (superfine) sugar
2 tablespoons orange-flavoured liqueur
¹/₂ cup (50g) cocoa nibs, optional

CHOCOLATE ORANGE MOUSSE
1 cup (250ml) milk
3 teaspoons finely grated orange rind
2¹/₂ teaspoons powdered gelatine
5 egg yolks
¹/₂ cup (110g) caster (superfine) sugar
¹/₄ cup (60ml) orange juice
200g (6¹/₂ ounces) milk chocolate (33% cocoa)
300ml thick (double) cream

MILK CHOCOLATE SAUCE
180g (5¹/₂ ounces) milk chocolate (33% cocoa), chopped finely
1 cup (250ml) pouring cream

1 Preheat oven to 180°C/350°F. Grease a deep 20cm (8-inch) springform pan; line base and side with baking paper.
2 Stir chocolate and butter in a small heavy-based saucepan over low heat until smooth. Cool for 10 minutes. Beat egg yolks and sugar in a small bowl with an electric mixer for 5 minutes or until thick and pale. Beat in chocolate mixture until combined. Transfer mixture to a large bowl. Beat egg whites in a small bowl with an electric mixer until soft peaks form; fold into chocolate mixture, in two batches. Pour mixture into pan.
3 Bake cake for 20 minutes or until cake is just firm to touch. Cool in pan.
4 Meanwhile, make chocolate orange mousse.
5 Remove cake from pan. Wash and dry pan; grease then line base and side of pan with baking paper. Remove lining paper from cake; place cake, top-side down, back in pan. Press down firmly on cake to ensure it completely covers the base of the pan. Brush liqueur on cake; pour mousse over cake. Refrigerate 6 hours or overnight until set.
6 Make milk chocolate sauce.
7 Sprinkle cocoa nibs on cake, pour a little warm sauce over the top. Serve cake immediately with remaining sauce.

CHOCOLATE ORANGE MOUSSE Place milk and rind in a small heavy-based saucepan; bring almost to the boil. Sprinkle gelatine over milk mixture; whisk until gelatine dissolves. Beat egg yolks and sugar in a small bowl with an electric mixer for 3 minutes or until thick and pale. Beat in juice. Gradually beat in hot milk mixture. Return mixture to same pan; cook, stirring continuously, over medium-low heat until mixture thickens enough to coat the back of spoon (don't boil or mixture will curdle). Add chocolate; stand for 1 minute, then whisk until chocolate has melted. Strain mixture through a fine sieve into a clean bowl; cool for 1 hour, stirring occasionally. Beat cream in a small bowl with an electric mixer until soft peaks form. Fold cream into chocolate mixture; use immediately.

MILK CHOCOLATE SAUCE Stir chocolate and cream in a small heavy-based saucepan over low heat until smooth.

TIPS Cocoa nibs are created in the early stage of chocolate production. Cocoa beans are dried then roasted, after which they are crushed into what are termed 'nibs'. Next, the nibs are ground to separate cocoa butter and cocoa solids. Nibs are both textural and chocolatey with no sweetness. They can be found at health food stores and specialist food stores. To cut neat slices from the cake, wipe the knife with paper towel between each cut.
TECHNIQUES Step 4: see also *'dissolving powdered gelatine'*, page 277.
DO-AHEAD The cake can be made a day ahead; store in an airtight container in the refrigerator.

[PHOTOGRAPH PAGES 26 & 27]

COCOA

DUTCH-PROCESSED COCOA SHOULD NOT BE SUBSTITUTED FOR ORDINARY 'NATURAL' COCOA IN A RECIPE THAT INCLUDES BICARBONATE OF SODA AS THE PRINCIPLE RAISING AGENT. THIS IS BECAUSE THE ACIDITY OF ORDINARY COCOA IS NEEDED TO REACT WITH THE ALKALINE BICARBONATE OF SODA TO CAUSE LEAVENING.

COCOA SOLIDS

PUT SIMPLY, THE PERCENTAGE OF COCOA SOLIDS LISTED ON A CHOCOLATE LABEL TELLS YOU TWO THINGS: HOW SWEET THE CHOCOLATE IS AND HOW INTENSE THE CHOCOLATE TASTES. THE HIGHER THE PERCENTAGE, THE LESS SWEET THE CHOCOLATE AND MORE INTENSE THE TASTE. CHOCOLATE WITH 70 PERCENT COCOA SOLIDS, ALSO KNOWN AS BITTERSWEET, IS CONSIDERED HIGH, THOUGH IT IS ALSO AVAILABLE FROM THE SUPERMARKET WITH UP TO 85 PERCENT COCOA SOLIDS.

DUTCH-PROCESSED COCOA *refers to cocoa that has had an alkaline added, during a process called 'dutching' – which was perfected in Holland. The resulting cocoa has a richer chocolate taste and colour.*

CHOPPING *Chocolate*

It's much easier to chop chocolate with a serrated knife, rather than a cook's knife which tends to slip – serrations will provide better traction. For finely chopped chocolate, try using a food processor – chop in small batches, using the pulse button, otherwise the blades can overheat and melt the chocolate.

INSTANT GANACHE

Rather than waiting for a ganache to cool to a spreadable consistency, add finely chopped chocolate off the heat to almost boiling cream; the chocolate will melt, cooling the chocolate so it's instantly useable.

Chocolate BLOOM

Chocolate is sensitive to heat so store it in a cool place but not the fridge. Chocolate that has been subjected to changes in temperature can discolour and develop what is known as 'chocolate bloom', however it can still be used in baking.

COCOA NIBS

ARE CREATED IN THE EARLY STAGE OF CHOCOLATE PRODUCTION. COCOA BEANS ARE DRIED THEN ROASTED, AFTER WHICH THEY ARE CRUSHED INTO WHAT ARE TERMED 'NIBS'. NEXT, THE NIBS ARE GROUND TO SEPARATE COCOA BUTTER AND COCOA SOLIDS. NIBS ARE BOTH TEXTURAL AND CHOCOLATEY WITH NO SWEETNESS. THEY CAN BE FOUND AT HEALTH FOOD STORES AND SPECIALIST FOOD STORES.

MILK CHOCOLATE *Seek out a milk chocolate with at least 33 percent cocoa solids so you get some chocolate flavour in your cake not just sweetness. Look in the confectionery section of the supermarket rather than the baking aisle.*

TROUBLE SHOOTING

If a little water gets into chocolate that is being melted the cocoa particles stick together and the chocolate becomes stiff or 'seizes up'. If the chocolate is to be added to a cake, it is actually okay to add a greater quantity of water to loosen the particles. Try stirring in 1-2 tablespoons water to loosen it. If the chocolate is to be used on its own then you're better to start over.

DID YOU KNOW

WHITE CHOCOLATE, STRICTLY SPEAKING, ISN'T CHOCOLATE AT ALL. IT CONTAINS NO COCOA SOLIDS OR CHOCOLATE TASTE, JUST FAT, SUGAR AND MILK SOLIDS.

Cookies-and-cream cake

PREP + COOK TIME **1 HOUR 15 MINUTES (+ REFRIGERATION)** SERVES **10**

250g (8 ounces) butter, softened

1 teaspoon vanilla bean paste

1¼ cups (275g) caster (superfine) sugar

3 eggs

2¼ cups (335g) self-raising flour

¼ cup (35g) plain (all-purpose) flour

¾ cup (180ml) milk

150g (4½ ounces) Oreo biscuits, chopped coarsely

5 Oreo biscuits (55g), extra, chopped

CRÈME PÂTISSIÈRE

3 cups (750ml) milk

1½ teaspoons vanilla bean paste

6 egg yolks

½ cup (110g) caster (superfine) sugar

⅓ cup (50g) cornflour (cornstarch)

60g (2 ounces) butter

200g (6½ ounces) dark (semi-sweet) chocolate, chopped

1 Preheat oven to 180°C/350°F. Grease a deep 20cm (8-inch) round cake pan; line base and sides with three layers of baking paper, extending the paper 2cm (¾-inch) above top.

2 Beat butter, paste and sugar in a medium bowl with an electric mixer until pale and fluffy. Beat in eggs, one at a time. Stir in sifted flours and milk, in two batches. Stir in chopped biscuits. Spread mixture into pan; smooth surface.

3 Bake cake for 1 hour or until a skewer inserted into the centre comes out clean. Stand cake in pan for 5 minutes before turning, top-side up, onto a wire rack to cool.

4 Meanwhile, make crème pâtissière.

5 Split cake into three layers. Whisk each crème pâtissière mixture until smooth. Place the bottom cake layer on a cake stand or plate; spread with half the chocolate crème pâtissière. Top with middle cake layer; spread with plain crème pâtissière. Finish with top cake layer and remaining chocolate crème pâtissière. Decorate with extra chopped biscuits.

CRÈME PÂTISSIÈRE Heat milk and paste in a small saucepan over medium heat until almost boiling. Whisk yolks, sugar and cornflour in a medium bowl; gradually whisk in hot milk mixture. Return mixture to pan; whisk over low heat for 5 minutes or until mixture boils and thickens. Remove from heat; stir in 40g (1½ ounces) of the butter. Reserve one-third of the mixture in a small bowl. Stir chocolate and remaining butter into remaining mixture until melted through. Cover bowls; refrigerate until cold.

TECHNIQUES Step 1: see *'lining a round cake pan'*, page 276. Step 5: see *'splitting a cake into even layers'*, page 277.
DO-AHEAD The cake and crème pâtissière can be made a day ahead. Store cake in an airtight container at room temperature; refrigerate crème pâtissière, covered tightly.

Peanut butter
CHOCOLATE CAKE

PREP + COOK TIME 1 HOUR 30 MINUTES (+ REFRIGERATION) SERVES 12

1/2 cup (50g) dutch-processed cocoa

1/2 cup (125ml) boiling water

185g (6 ounces) butter, softened

11/2 cups (330g) caster (superfine) sugar

1 teaspoon vanilla extract

3 eggs

1/4 cup (70g) smooth peanut butter

11/2 cups (225g) self-raising flour

1/2 cup (75g) plain (all-purpose) flour

3/4 cup (180ml) buttermilk

220g (7 ounces) peanut-butter-filled milk chocolate (33% cocoa), chopped coarsely

PEANUT BUTTER GANACHE

360g (111/2 ounces) white chocolate, chopped

2 tablespoons smooth peanut butter

1/2 cup (125ml) pouring cream

1 Preheat oven to 180°C/350°F. Grease a deep 20cm (8-inch) square cake pan; line base and sides with baking paper.

2 Stir cocoa and the water in a small heatproof jug until cocoa dissolves. Cool 10 minutes.

3 Beat butter, sugar and extract in a small bowl with an electric mixer until pale and fluffy. Beat in eggs, one at a time, then cocoa mixture and peanut butter until combined (mixture may look curdled at this stage). Beat in sifted dry ingredients and buttermilk, in two batches, until smooth. Spread mixture into pan.

4 Bake cake for 11/4 hours or until a skewer inserted into the centre comes out clean. Stand cake in pan 5 minutes before turning, top-side up, onto a wire rack to cool.

5 Meanwhile, make peanut butter ganache.

6 Beat cold peanut butter ganache with an electric mixer until pale and fluffy. Spread ganache on top of cooled cake; top with peanut-butter-filled chocolate.

PEANUT BUTTER GANACHE Place chocolate and peanut butter in a medium heatproof bowl. Heat cream in a small saucepan until almost boiling; pour over chocolate mixture, whisking until smooth. Cover; refrigerate for 1 hour, stirring occasionally until mixture is chilled and thickened.

TECHNIQUES Step 1: see *'lining a square cake pan'*, page 276.
DO-AHEAD The cake can be made up to 3 days ahead; store in an airtight container at room temperature. The peanut butter ganache is best made on the day of serving.

Chocolate
RICOTTA CHEESECAKE
with candied fruit

PREP + COOK TIME 1 HOUR 45 MINUTES (+ COOLING & STANDING) SERVES 12

180g (5½ ounces) dark (semi-sweet) chocolate, chopped
180g (5½ ounces) unsalted butter, softened
1⅓ cups (300g) caster (superfine) sugar
3 eggs
1 cup (120g) ground almonds
½ cup (75g) plain (all-purpose) flour
¼ cup (25g) dutch-processed cocoa
400g (12½ ounces) glacé clementines, halved or quartered

RICOTTA CHEESECAKE LAYER
250g (8 ounces) cream cheese, softened
400g (12½ ounces) ricotta
⅔ cup (150g) caster (superfine) sugar
3 eggs
2 tablespoons orange-flavoured liqueur
100g (3 ounces) glacé clementines or orange, chopped
2 tablespoons finely chopped glacé citron (cedro)

CHOCOLATE GANACHE
½ cup (125ml) pouring cream
180g (5½ ounces) dark (semi-sweet) chocolate, chopped

1 Make ricotta cheesecake layer.
2 Preheat oven to 160°C/325°F. Grease a 25cm (10-inch) springform pan; line base and side with baking paper.
3 Stir chocolate in a small heatproof bowl over a small saucepan of simmering water (don't let water touch base of bowl) until smooth; cool 10 minutes.

4 Meanwhile, beat butter and sugar in a small bowl with an electric mixer for 5 minutes or until pale and fluffy. Beat in eggs, one at a time, until just combined. Stir in ground almonds, sifted flour and cocoa, and melted chocolate. Spread chocolate mixture into pan. Pour ricotta cheesecake layer over chocolate layer.
5 Bake cheesecake for 1 hour 5 minutes or until slightly wobbly in the centre. Cool in oven with the door ajar.
6 Make chocolate ganache.
7 Place cheesecake on a plate or cake stand. Spread ganache on top of cake; decorate with clementines. Stand until set or refrigerate 30 minutes.

RICOTTA CHEESECAKE LAYER Beat cream cheese in a small bowl with an electric mixer until smooth. Add ricotta and sugar; beat for 2 minutes or until smooth. Add eggs and liqueur; beat until just combined. Stir in glacé fruit.

CHOCOLATE GANACHE Bring cream almost to the boil in a small saucepan; remove from heat. Add chocolate; stir until smooth. Stand 15 minutes or until ganache is spreadable.

TIPS You can substitute glacé fruit with others of your choice. Cut the cake with a hot knife. Wipe the blade clean between cuts.
TECHNIQUES Step 3: see also *'melting chocolate'*, page 277.
DO-AHEAD The cheesecake will have a softer texture if made on the day of serving, however it can be made a day ahead; store, covered in the fridge.

Gooey *bready* with notes of *cinnamon* drizzled with a warm *mocha glaze*

Chocolate and cinnamon babka
[RECIPE PAGES 40 & 41]

CHOCOLATE AND CINNAMON *Babka*

PREP + COOK TIME 1 HOUR 20 MINUTES (+ STANDING) SERVES 8

$^1/_2$ cup (80g) sultanas

$^1/_3$ cup (80ml) coffee-flavoured liqueur

$^3/_4$ cup (180ml) lukewarm milk

4 teaspoons (14g) dried yeast

$^1/_2$ cup (110g) caster (superfine) sugar

2 eggs, beaten lightly

1 egg yolk

3 cups (450g) '00' flour, bread flour or plain (all-purpose) flour

3 teaspoons sea salt flakes

150g ($4^1/_2$ ounces) butter, softened, cubed

40g ($1^1/_2$ ounces) butter, extra, softened

200g ($6^1/_2$ ounces) dark (semi-sweet) chocolate, chopped

$^1/_2$ cup pouring cream

$^1/_4$ cup (35g) coarsely chopped walnuts

FILLING

$^2/_3$ cup (70g) walnuts, roasted lightly, chopped

$^1/_3$ cup (75g) firmly packed brown sugar

2 teaspoons ground cinnamon

150g ($4^1/_2$ ounces) dark (semi-sweet) chocolate, chopped coarsely

1 Combine sultanas and liqueur in a small bowl; set aside.

2 Combine milk, yeast and 1 tablespoon of the sugar in a small bowl; cover with plastic wrap. Stand bowl in a warm place for 10 minutes or until frothy. Stir in eggs and yolk.

3 Place flour, salt, remaining sugar and yeast mixture in a large bowl of an electric mixer fitted with a dough hook attachment. Mix on low speed until just combined, then medium speed for 5 minutes or until soft and elastic. With motor operating, gradually add cubed butter, a piece at a time, making sure the butter is incorporated before adding the next piece. Mix until dough is very smooth and elastic. Place dough in a large oiled bowl; cover with plastic wrap. Stand in a warm place for 1 hour or until dough doubles in size (the temperature should not be too warm or the butter will melt and the dough will be greasy).

4 Meanwhile, combine filling ingredients in a small bowl.

5 Preheat oven to 200°C/400°F. Grease a non-stick 21cm ($8^1/_2$-inch) kugelhopf pan well with some butter. Drain sultanas; reserve 2 tablespoons of the liqueur.

6 Punch down dough with your fist. Knead lightly until smooth. Roll dough out on a piece of floured baking paper into a 30cm x 45cm (12-inch x 18-inch) rectangle until 1cm ($^1/_2$-inch) thick.

7 Spread dough with extra butter. Sprinkle evenly with liqueur-soaked sultanas and filling mixture. Using paper as an aide, roll up firmly from one long side. Using a lightly oiled knife, cut the dough into 12 equal pieces (reshape pieces into rounds); place seven pieces cut-side out, around the outer side of the pan (use the middle pieces of the log for this). Place remaining end pieces of the log around the ring of the pan, overlapping slightly; cover with plastic wrap. Stand pan in a warm place for 45 minutes or until dough has almost doubled.

8 Bake babka on the lowest oven shelf for 40 minutes or until dough is cooked through. Stand for 5 minutes before, turning top-side down, onto a wire rack to cool slightly.

9 Place dark chocolate, cream and reserved liqueur in a medium microwave-safe bowl; microwave on HIGH for 1 minute or until melted and smooth. Cool 10 minutes.

10 Serve warm babka drizzled with warm sauce.

TIP Both '00' and bread flour have a higher protein content (12.5–14%) than regular plain (all-purpose) flour (10–12%), and it is this extra gluten protein which gives bread and yeasted cakes their structure. Both flours are sold alongside regular flour in supermarkets.

TO MAKE DOUGH BY HAND In step 3, combine ingredients in a large bowl with a wooden spoon to form a soft dough. Turn out onto a well-floured surface and knead for 5 minutes or until soft and elastic. Knead butter, piece by piece, into dough kneading well after each addition until all butter is incorporated and dough is smooth and elastic. Continue with instructions in step 3.

DO-AHEAD The babka is best made on day of serving.

[PHOTOGRAPH PAGES 38 & 39]

CHOCOLATE AND CINNAMON *Babka*

[RECIPE PAGES 40 & 41]

ACTIVATING THE YEAST MIXTURE

Place lukewarm milk (that is milk that you could comfortably hold your finger in) with yeast and sugar in a small bowl. Stand the mix 10 minutes until frothy. This step tells you if the yeast is active. If no bubbles appear, it is inactive and it could be that the yeast is out of date, in which case you will need to start again with fresh yeast.

MAKING THE DOUGH

Make sure that the butter that is added to the dough is neither too soft, nor too cold. If it is too cold it will be hard to incorporate; if it's too soft, the dough will become greasy. To gauge if the butter is just right, push it gently with your finger; it should leave an impression on the surface.

FILLING THE DOUGH

If the dough feels too soft to roll, which might happen on a hot day, place it in the fridge until firmer. To help roll the dough to the measurements given, use a ruler or other straight-sided object to ensure that the edges are straight.

CUTTING THE DOUGH

Cut the dough using an oiled knife, trying not to apply pressure to the dough itself, instead use a fast sawing action. An easy way to cut the dough into 12 equal pieces, is to cut it in half first, then each half in half again, and finally each quarter into three.

FILLING THE PAN

Place dough pieces in the order instructed in the recipe so that they fit evenly into the pan. This will give the babka dough a swirled effect when it is sliced.

SERVING

The babka is best served warm. Cut with a serrated knife. It also freezes well. Thaw overnight in the fridge. To reheat, wrap the babka in foil and place in a 180°C/350°F oven for 15 minutes or until warmed through. Drizzle with sauce.

MUSCATEL
brownie cake
with fudge icing

PREP + COOK TIME **1 HOUR 20 MINUTES (+ COOLING)** SERVES **10**

200g (6^1/$_2$ ounces) dried muscatels on the vine

1 cup (250ml) muscat or tokay

250g (8 ounces) butter, chopped

500g (1 pound) dark (semi-sweet) chocolate, chopped

1 cup (220g) firmly packed brown sugar

3 eggs

1^1/$_2$ cups (225g) plain (all-purpose) flour

1 cup (150g) self-raising flour

^{1}/$_3$ cup (80g) sour cream

2 tablespoons caster (superfine) sugar

FUDGE ICING

250g (8 ounces) dark (semi-sweet) chocolate

^{1}/$_2$ cup (120g) sour cream

^{1}/$_4$ cup (40g) icing (confectioners') sugar

1 Remove seeds from half the muscatels; place in a small bowl. Place remaining muscatels on the vine in another small bowl. Place muscat in a small saucepan over medium heat; bring to the boil. Pour hot muscat equally between the bowls; stand for 30 minutes. Strain seeded muscatels over muscatels on the vine.

2 Preheat oven 160°C/325°F. Grease a 20cm (8-inch) square cake pan; line base and sides with baking paper.

3 Melt butter in a medium saucepan over low heat; stir in chocolate until smooth. Remove from heat; stir in brown sugar. Cool 10 minutes. Whisk eggs into chocolate mixture. Stir in seeded muscatels until coated in mixture, then stir in flours and sour cream. Pour mixture into pan; smooth the surface.

4 Bake cake for 1 hour 10 minutes or until top is firm and a skewer inserted in the centre comes out with moist crumbs attached. Cool in pan.

5 Meanwhile, drain remaining muscatels over a small saucepan; reserve muscatels. Add caster sugar to pan; bring to the boil, stirring until sugar dissolves. Reduce heat; simmer for 5 minutes or until syrup thickens. Add muscatels on the vine; simmer for 1 minute. Cool.

6 Make fudge icing.

7 Spread frosting on cooled cake. Top with muscatels; drizzle with syrup.

FUDGE ICING Place chocolate in a heatproof medium bowl over a medium saucepan of simmer water (don't allow bowl to touch water); stir until just melted. Add sour cream, then gradually add sifted icing sugar, stirring until smooth.

TIP Muscat and tokay are both fortified wines available from liquor stores. You can also use sweet sherry or port.

TECHNIQUES Step 2: see *'lining a square cake pan'*, page 276. Step 6: see also *'melting chocolate'*, page 277.

DO-AHEAD The brownie can be made a day ahead; store in an airtight container at room temperature.

Oranges & LEMONS

CITRUSY BURSTS OF
Oranges
and Lemons
bring the
Sunshine
TO ALL THEY TOUCH

PISTACHIO AND lemon curd cake

PREP + COOK TIME 1 HOUR 20 MINUTES (+ REFRIGERATION) SERVES 12

1¼ cups (160g) finely chopped pistachios
125g (4 ounces) unsalted butter
1 cup (220g) caster (superfine) sugar
1 tablespoon finely grated lemon rind
3 eggs
²/₃ cup (100g) cake flour
1 teaspoon baking powder

LEMON CURD
3 eggs
1½ tablespoons finely grated lemon rind
½ cup (125ml) lemon juice
¾ cup (165g) caster (superfine) sugar
100g (3½ ounces) unsalted butter

1 Make lemon curd.
2 Preheat oven to 180°C/350°F. Grease a 22cm (9-inch) springform pan; line base and side with two layers of baking paper. Spray the side lining paper with oil, avoiding the base. Place ¼ cup (45g) of the nuts in the pan; rotate pan on its side to coat side with nuts.
3 Beat butter, sugar and rind in a medium bowl with an electric mixer for 3 minutes until pale and fluffy. Beat in eggs, one at a time, until combined.
4 Sift flour and baking powder into a small bowl, add ²/₃ cup (90g) of the nuts; stir to combine. Using a large metal spoon, fold dry ingredients into egg mixture until just combined.

5 Spoon cake mixture into pan; drop pan on work surface to settle the mixture. Spread 1 cup (200g) of the curd over batter, levelling the surface; scatter evenly with remaining pistachios. Cover remaining curd; refrigerate.
6 Bake cake for 40 minutes; cover surface with a round of baking paper to prevent nuts burning, then bake a further 10 minutes or until a skewer inserted into the centre comes out clean (the top will still be slightly wobbly). Serve cake warm or at room temperature with remaining lemon curd.

LEMON CURD Combine eggs, rind, juice and sugar in a medium heatproof bowl; set over a medium saucepan of simmering water. Stir about 10 minutes or until mixture thickens and thickly coats the back of a spoon. Gradually add butter, stirring until smooth between additions. Strain mixture into a medium bowl. Cover surface with plastic wrap; cool. Refrigerate for 3 hours or until chilled.

TIPS You can finely chop the pistachios in a food processor if you like; use the pulse button, in bursts, for an even texture. Cake flour is lower in protein than plain (all-purpose) flour so it produces a finer, more tender crumb in baking. It is best to use freshly squeezed lemon juice in the lemon curd.
DO-AHEAD The curd can be made up to 1 week ahead; store in an airtight container in the refrigerator. The cake is best made on the day of serving.

Lemon cake
WITH MASCARPONE FROSTING

PREP + COOK TIME **1 HOUR 45 MINUTES (+ STANDING)** SERVES **12**

225g (7 ounces) butter, softened
1¹/₂ tablespoons finely grated lemon rind
1 cup (220g) caster (superfine) sugar
3 eggs
¹/₂ cup (160g) store-bought lemon curd
1¹/₂ cup (225g) self-raising flour
³/₄ cup (110g) plain (all-purpose) flour
¹/₄ teaspoon salt
1 cup (250ml) milk

SESAME SEED CRUNCH
¹/₃ cup (75g) caster (superfine) sugar
1¹/₂ tablespoons water
2 teaspoons sesame seeds, toasted

MASCARPONE FROSTING
300ml thickened (heavy) cream
250g (8 ounces) mascarpone, at room temperature
2 teaspoons icing (confectioners') sugar

1 Preheat oven to 180°C/350°F. Grease a deep 25cm (10-inch) fluted tube cake pan.
2 Beat butter, rind and sugar in a small bowl with an electric mixer until pale and fluffy. Beat in eggs, one at a time, until just combined. Fold in curd, sifted flours, salt and milk. Spoon mixture into pan.
3 Bake cake for 45 minutes or until a skewer inserted into the centre comes out clean. Stand cake in pan for 15 minutes before turning out onto a wire rack to cool.

4 Meanwhile, make sesame seed crunch.
5 Make mascarpone frosting.
6 Level base of the cake if necessary (see TECHNIQUES), then place on a platter. Spoon half the frosting on cake; decorate with sesame seed crunch. Serve cake with remaining frosting.

SESAME SEED CRUNCH Line an oven tray with baking paper. Stir sugar and the water in a small saucepan over medium heat until sugar dissolves. Bring to the boil. Reduce heat; simmer until syrup turns a golden caramel (see TECHNIQUES). Immediately pour mixture onto tray. Sprinkle with sesame seeds. Stand until set. Finely chop a quarter of the crunch; break remainder into small pieces.

MASCARPONE FROSTING Beat ³/₄ cup (180ml) cream in a small bowl with an electric mixer until soft peaks form. Combine mascarpone and sifted icing sugar in a medium bowl; fold in whipped cream, then remaining cream.

TIP We have used store-bought lemon curd in this recipe but you can make your own using the recipe on page 50.
TECHNIQUES Step 4: see also *'making caramel and praline'*, page 277. Step 6: see *'levelling a cake'*, page 277.
DO-AHEAD The cake and sesame seed crunch can be made a day ahead; store separately in airtight containers at room temperature. The frosting is best made close to serving.

Whole orange semolina cake
WITH ROSEMARY SYRUP

PREP + COOK TIME 2 HOURS 40 MINUTES (+ STANDING) SERVES 12

2 large oranges (600g)
1 teaspoon baking powder
6 eggs
1 cup (220g) caster (superfine) sugar
1 cup (150g) fine semolina
1¼ cups (150g) ground almonds
1½ teaspoons finely chopped fresh rosemary leaves

ROSEMARY SYRUP
2 large oranges (600g)
½ cup (110g) caster (superfine) sugar
½ cup (125ml) water
1½ tablespoons lemon juice
2 tablespoons orange-flavoured liqueur
2 x 8cm (3¼-inch) sprigs fresh rosemary

1 Place unpeeled oranges in a medium saucepan over high heat, cover with cold water; bring to the boil. Boil, covered, 1½ hours or until oranges are tender; drain. Cool.
2 Preheat oven to 180°C/350°F. Grease a deep 22cm (9-inch) round cake pan; line base and side with baking paper.
3 Trim and discard ends from oranges. Halve oranges; discard seeds. Process orange, including rind, with baking powder until mixture is pulpy. Transfer to a large bowl.

4 Process eggs and sugar for 5 minutes or until thick and creamy. Stir egg mixture into orange mixture. Fold in semolina, ground almonds and rosemary. Spread mixture into pan.
5 Bake cake for 1 hour or until a skewer inserted into the centre comes out clean. Stand cake in pan for 45 minutes before turning, top-side up, onto a cake plate.
6 Make rosemary syrup.
7 Spoon hot syrup over warm cake. Serve cake warm or at room temperature.

ROSEMARY SYRUP Remove rind from 1 orange with a zester, into thin strips. Using a vegetable peeler, peel a long continuous strip of rind from remaining orange. Place sugar, the water and juice in a small saucepan over low heat; stir, without boiling, until sugar dissolves. Add long strip of rind, bring to the boil; boil for 5 minutes or until syrup thickens. Remove from heat; stir in liqueur, rosemary and thin strips of rind.

TIPS If you don't have a zester, simply peel the rind into wide strips with a vegetable peeler, then cut them into thin strips. You could vary the flavourings in the syrup by adding either a cinnamon stick or a split vanilla bean instead of rosemary.
TECHNIQUES Step 2: see *'lining a round cake pan'*, page 276.
DO-AHEAD The cake is best made on day of serving.

Lemon curd
AND POPPY SEED CRÊPE CAKE

PREP + COOK TIME 1 HOUR 30 MINUTES (+ REFRIGERATION, COOLING & STANDING) SERVES 8

1 cup (150g) plain (all-purpose) flour
4 eggs
1 tablespoon vegetable oil
2 cups (500ml) milk
1 tablespoon poppy seeds
500g (1 pound) mascarpone
50g (1½ ounces) store-bought meringues, crushed coarsely

LEMON CURD

1 titanium-strength gelatine leaf (5g)
3 eggs
4 egg yolks
2 teaspoons finely grated lemon rind
½ cup (125ml) lemon juice
1 cup (220g) caster (superfine) sugar
250g (8 ounces) butter, chopped

VANILLA BLUEBERRIES

1 vanilla bean
½ cup (110g) caster (superfine) sugar
¼ cup (60ml) water
5cm (2-inch) strip lemon rind
250g (8 ounces) blueberries

1 Make lemon curd.
2 Make vanilla blueberries.
3 Place flour in a medium bowl; make a well in the centre. Gradually whisk combined eggs, oil and milk into flour until smooth. Strain mixture into a large jug; stir in poppy seeds. Stand for 30 minutes.
4 Stir batter. Heat an oiled 20cm (8-inch) based frying pan; pour ¼ cup of the batter into pan, tilting the pan to coat base. Cook over low heat, loosening around edge with a spatula until browned lightly. Turn crêpe; brown other side. Repeat with remaining batter to make 15 crêpes; you need 14 for the stack.
5 Place 1 crêpe on a rimmed plate; spread with ⅓ cup lemon curd. Top with another crêpe; spread with ⅓ cup mascarpone. Repeat layering with 12 more crêpes, remaining lemon curd and mascarpone, finishing with a crêpe. As you layer use pieces of meringue to prop up the edges of the crêpe.
6 Serve crêpe cake topped with vanilla blueberries. Dust with icing (confectioners') sugar, if you like.

LEMON CURD Soften gelatine in a bowl of cold water 3 minutes; squeeze out excess water (see TECHNIQUES). Combine eggs, egg yolks, rind, juice and sugar in a medium heatproof bowl. Place bowl over a medium saucepan of simmering water (don't let the base of the bowl touch the water). Stir mixture 10 minutes or until it thickens and thickly coats the back of a spoon. Whisk in butter, a piece at a time, until smooth between additions. Stir in gelatine until dissolved. Cool. Refrigerate 3 hours or overnight.

VANILLA BLUEBERRIES Split vanilla bean lengthways; scrape seeds (see TECHNIQUES) into a small saucepan, then add bean. Add sugar, the water and rind; stir over low heat, without boiling, until sugar dissolves. Bring to the boil. Reduce heat; simmer for 3 minutes. Remove from heat; stir in blueberries. Cool.

TIP This batter makes 15 crêpes however the first crêpe seasons the pan and never looks that good. Stack the 14 best crêpes.
TECHNIQUES Step 1: see also *'dissolving gelatine leaves'*, page 277. Step 2: see also *'preparing vanilla beans'*, page 276.
DO-AHEAD Crêpes and lemon curd can be made a day ahead. Stack crêpes, layered with pieces of baking paper; place curd in an airtight container. Refrigerate both until ready to assemble.

Lemon curd
AND POPPY SEED CRÊPE CAKE

[RECIPE PAGE 57]

MAKING LEMON CURD
Ensure the bowl doesn't touch the simmering water and that the mixture doesn't get too hot or it will curdle. The lemon curd is ready when the mixture thickly coats the back of a wooden spoon.

MAKING VANILLA BLUEBERRIES
Split the vanilla bean and scrape out the seeds (see also *'preparing vanilla beans'*, page 276), or if you like, you can use 1 teaspoon vanilla extract or vanilla bean paste. Briefly cook vanilla with the other ingredients, just long enough for the blueberries to infuse their flavour into the syrup but still hold their shape.

MAKING THE CRÊPE BATTER
Whisk the crêpe batter ingredients together as instructed. Alternatively, combine the batter ingredients in a food processor; you won't need to strain the mixture before adding the poppy seeds. Resting the batter gives the gluten in the flour a chance to relax, resulting in tender-textured crêpes.

COOKING THE CRÊPES

If you have one, cook the crêpes in a crêpe pan; these pans have a heavy-base for even cooking and shallow sides for easy removal. A non-stick frying pan is also fine to use. As you cook the crêpes the pan will become increasingly hotter, so you will need to lower the heat to compensate, or it will become hard to swirl the batter and the crêpes might become too brown.

ASSEMBLING THE CRÊPE CAKE

Allow yourself about 20 minutes to assemble the crêpe cake. Use the pieces of meringue to prop up the crêpe edges and prevent them from drooping. If you need to, you can assemble up to 3 hours ahead without the blueberries; store the cake in the fridge. For the best flavour, remove from the fridge 30 minutes before serving.

SERVING

Cut the crêpe cake with a sharp, thin bladed knife. Always start by angling the point of the knife into the centre of the cake. After cutting a couple of slices, wipe the blade clean with paper towel; this will help to keep the slices clean and neat.

Lime and passionfruit frozen yoghurt cake
[RECIPE PAGES 62 & 63]

Lime and passionfruit FROZEN YOGHURT CAKE

PREP + COOK TIME 1 HOUR 15 MINUTES (+ COOLING & FREEZING) SERVES 12

You will need to make this recipe the day before.

³/₄ cup (110g) plain (all-purpose) flour

¹/₄ cup (35g) self-raising flour

¹/₂ teaspoon bicarbonate of soda (baking soda)

2 teaspoons finely grated lime rind

¹/₃ cup (90g) firmly packed grated palm sugar

65g (2 ounces) butter

¹/₃ cup (115g) golden syrup or treacle

1 egg

¹/₂ cup (125ml) buttermilk

1¹/₂ cups (420g) Greek-style yoghurt

300ml thickened (heavy) cream

²/₃ cup (160ml) passionfruit pulp

CANDIED LIMES

1¹/₂ cups (305g) firmly packed grated palm sugar

¹/₂ cup (125ml) water

2 tablespoons lime juice

1 stalk fresh lemon grass, quartered, bruised

4 limes, peeled, sliced thinly

1 Make candied limes.

2 Preheat oven to 170°C/340°F. Grease a 26cm x 32cm (10¹/₂-inch x 12³/₄-inch) swiss roll pan; line base and long sides with baking paper, extending the paper 5cm (2 inches) over the sides.

3 Sift flours and soda into a medium bowl; stir in rind. Stir sugar, butter and golden syrup in a small saucepan over low heat until sugar dissolves. Stir warm butter mixture, egg and buttermilk into flour mixture. Pour mixture into pan.

4 Bake cake for 12 minutes or until cake springs back when pressed lightly with a finger and shrinks away from side of pan slightly. Brush warm cake with 2 tablespoons of the reserved candied lime syrup. Cool in pan.

5 Line the base and sides of a deep 14cm x 23cm (5¹/₂-inch x 9¹/₄-inch) loaf pan with baking paper. Arrange lime slices, overlapping slightly, on base of pan.

6 Beat yoghurt and cream in a small bowl with an electric mixer until soft peaks form; fold in all but 1 tablespoon of the remaining reserved candied lime syrup and half the passionfruit. Carefully pour a little more than one-third of yoghurt mixture into loaf pan (this will be about 1½ cups of mixture). Trim 12cm x 22cm (4¾-inch x 9-inch) piece from half the cake; carefully place in pan over yoghurt. Cover pan; freeze 1 hour or until firm. Refrigerate remaining yoghurt mixture. Cover remaining cake.
7 Pour remaining yoghurt mixture into pan. Trim a 14cm x 23cm (5½-inch x 9¼-inch) piece from remaining cake; carefully place on yoghurt layer. Cover; freeze for 3 hours or overnight.
8 Turn cake onto a platter; stand 10 minutes before serving. Just before serving, brush lime slices with remaining tablespoon of reserved candied lime syrup, drizzle with remaining passionfruit pulp.

[PHOTOGRAPH PAGES 60 & 61]

CANDIED LIMES Stir palm sugar, the water, juice and lemon grass in a medium heavy-based saucepan over low heat, without boiling, until sugar dissolves. Bring to the boil. Reduce heat; simmer, for 3 minutes or until syrup is reduced. Remove from heat; add lime slices and leave to cool in syrup. Drain lime slices; reserve slices and syrup separately. Discard lemon grass.

TIPS You will need about 8 passionfruit for this recipe. You can substitute canned passionfruit pulp, if you like, however to compensate for the sugar added during canning add a teaspoon or two of lime juice.
VARIATION For a lime and mango frozen yoghurt cake, use 1 cup pureed mango instead of the passionfruit in step 6 and decorate the top with mango slices instead of the remaining passionfruit in step 8.
DO-AHEAD Cake can be made up to 1 week head and frozen.

Upside-down mandarin polenta YOGHURT CAKE

PREP + COOK TIME 1 HOUR 5 MINUTES (+ COOLING) SERVES 16

5 small seedless mandarins (500g)

2 cups (440g) caster (superfine) sugar

1 cup (250ml) water

125g (4 ounces) unsalted butter

3 eggs

1 tablespoon finely grated mandarin rind

1 cup (170g) fine polenta

3/4 cup (165g) caster (superfine) sugar, extra

1 cup (280g) Greek-style yoghurt

1 1/2 cups (180g) ground almonds

1 1/2 teaspoons baking powder

MANDARIN YOGHURT

1/4 cup (55g) caster (superfine) sugar

1/4 cup (60ml) mandarin juice

1 cup (280g) Greek-style yoghurt

2 teaspoons finely grated orange rind

1 Preheat oven to 180°C/350°F. Grease a 20cm (8-inch) square cake pan; line with baking paper.

2 Peel mandarins then scrape away white pith from the outside of the fruit; separate into segments. Arrange segments in alternating rows over base of pan.

3 Stir sugar and the water in a medium saucepan over low heat, without boiling, until sugar dissolves. Bring to the boil; boil without stirring, for 10 minutes or until mixture turns a golden caramel (see TECHNIQUES). Quickly pour half the caramel over mandarin segments. Cool remaining caramel in saucepan (don't worry that the caramel hardens on cooling, you reheat it later).

4 Beat butter, eggs, rind, polenta and extra sugar in a large bowl with an electric mixer until pale and fluffy. Stir in yoghurt and combined sifted ground almonds and baking powder. Spoon mixture over mandarins and caramel in pan.

5 Bake cake for 1 hour or until golden and a skewer inserted into the centre comes out clean. Stand cake in pan for 5 minutes before turning out onto a cake plate; cool until just warm.

6 Meanwhile, make mandarin yoghurt

7 Just before serving, heat remaining caramel over low heat, without stirring, until melted. Taking care, pour hot caramel over top of cake. Serve with mandarin yoghurt.

MANDARIN YOGHURT Stir sugar and juice in a small saucepan over low heat, without boiling, until sugar dissolves. Bring to the boil; boil without stirring for 3 minutes or until syrup reduces slightly. Cool. Combine yoghurt, rind and cooled syrup in a small bowl. Cover; refrigerate until needed.

TIPS You will need a total of 8 mandarins for this recipe. Mandarins are softer than oranges and lemons which makes finely grating the rind a little trickier than usual; try using a microplane grater if you have one.

TECHNIQUES Step 1: see *'lining a square cake pan'*, page 276. Step 3: see also *'making caramel and praline'*, page 277.

DO-AHEAD This cake is best made on day of serving.

USE THE REAL DEAL

DON'T BE TEMPTED TO BUY READY-SQUEEZED JUICE, AS IT WILL LACK THE NATURAL ZING OF FRESHLY SQUEEZED JUICE, AND IN THE CASE OF LEMON JUICE CAN HAVE AN UNPLEASANT AFTERTASTE.

Electric MIXER

A HAND-HELD ELECTRIC MIXER DOES THE JOB OF MIXING CAKE BATTERS QUITE WELL, PROVIDING YOU MOVE THE MIXER AROUND THE BOWL TO ENSURE EVEN BEATING. A STAND MIXER WITH PLANETARY MOTION (I.E. THE ATTACHMENTS MOVE AROUND THE BOWL) IS MORE EFFICIENT, ESPECIALLY FOR MIXTURES SUCH AS FLUFFY ICING OR MERINGUE THAT REQUIRE BEATING FOR UP TO 10 MINUTES. STAND MIXERS ALSO MAKE EASY WORK OF MIXING STIFF YEASTED DOUGHS WITH A DOUGH HOOK ATTACHMENT.

JUICING *TO MAXIMISE THE YIELD OF JUICE, ESPECIALLY FROM LEMONS AND LIMES, ROLL THEM ON A COUNTER, APPLYING FIRM PRESSURE TO SOFTEN THEM SLIGHTLY AND ASSIST IN RELEASING THEIR JUICE.*

GRATED RIND

The outer rind (or zest) of citrus fruit has the most aroma. You can actually see the pore-like oil glands, especially in mandarins. Beneath this lies the white pith, which is to be avoided when peeling and grating as it is bitter.

VALENCIA ORANGES

The greenish-orange skin of Valencias can be attributed to summer's warm nights and days which cause a concentration of chlorophyll on the skin. In fact the greener the flesh, the sweeter the juice in this variety which is the best type for juicing.

OTHER CITRUS

A tangelo is a cross between a mandarin and a grapefruit. Try substituting it in recipes with orange, lemon or mandarin in them, for both sweetness and tang. Another wonderful hybrid is lemonade fruit, an orange/lemon cross; use similarly to tangelo. There are nine common mandarin varieties in Australia, some seedless, some not, and with varying levels of sweetness and acidity. For the nicest flavoured rind for cakes, early season imperial mandarins are best.

KNOW YOUR OVEN

Here's a scary thought – most domestic ovens are off by quite a few degrees, which impacts on cooking time. It's a good idea to have an oven thermometer that sits in the oven so you can see it. If your oven is off by 50 degrees it is definitely time to call in the professionals and get it recalibrated. Also, ovens can have hot spots; these can be dealt with by rotating items halfway through the cooking time.

GRATING GREATS

WHEN GRATING CITRUS USE THE SMALLEST HOLES ON A BOX GRATER TO ENSURE YOU'RE REMOVING THE ZEST OF THE RIND AND NOT THE BITTER PITH AS WELL. IT CAN BE HARD TO SCRAPE THE FINE RIND OFF THE GRATER. TO HELP, COVER THE GRATER WITH BAKING PAPER PUSHING IT OVER THE HOLES BEFORE YOU START GRATING. THEN, SIMPLY LIFT OFF THE PAPER WITH THE COLLECTED RIND. YOU COULD ALSO USE A MICROPLANE GRATER.

WAXED FRUIT *Most citrus fruit is waxed to look more appealing and to increase shelf-life. If you plan to use the rind, wash and rub it to remove the wax. Organic shops sell unwaxed fruit and some countries are starting to give the consumer a choice between unwaxed and waxed fruit.*

Citrus SEASONS

Winter and early spring is peak season for Australian citrus fruits. Navel oranges, mandarins, tangelos and lemons are all abundant then. Summer is the season for the green/orange-skinned valencia, while limes are best from mid-summer to mid-autumn.

THINK AHEAD

If a recipe calls for the juice only of a citrus fruit, don't waste the rind. Finely grate the rind before juicing. Place 1 teaspoon grated rind in each hole of an ice-cube tray; freeze for later use.

Blood orange cakes with mascarpone ice-cream
[RECIPE PAGES 70 & 71]

Blood orange cakes with
MASCARPONE ICE-CREAM

PREP + COOK TIME **2 HOURS 10 MINUTES (+ COOLING & FREEZING)** MAKES **8**

1¼ cups (185g) self-raising flour

½ teaspoon bicarbonate of soda (baking soda)

1 cup (120g) ground almonds

1¼ cups (275g) caster (superfine) sugar

½ cup (125ml) extra virgin olive oil

1 tablespoon finely grated blood orange rind

½ cup (125ml) strained freshly squeezed blood orange juice

3 eggs, beaten lightly

CANDIED BLOOD ORANGES

1½ cups (375ml) water

½ cup (125ml) strained freshly squeezed blood orange juice

1 cup (220g) caster (superfine) sugar

3 medium blood oranges (480g), cut into 5mm (¼-inch) slices

MASCARPONE ICE-CREAM

1 cup (250ml) strained freshly squeezed blood orange juice

300ml thickened (heavy) cream

1½ cups (240g) icing (confectioners') sugar

250g (8 ounces) mascarpone

1 Make candied blood oranges.

2 Make mascarpone ice-cream.

3 Preheat oven to 180°C/350°F. Grease eight 10cm (4-inch) springform pans. Line each base and side with baking paper.

4 Sift flour and soda into a large bowl; whisk in ground almonds and sugar. Add oil, rind, juice and eggs; whisk until mixture is smooth. Divide mixture into pans.

5 Bake cakes for 30 minutes or until a skewer inserted into the centre comes out clean. Stand cakes in pan for 5 minutes before transferring to plates.

6 Brush hot cakes with reserved syrup from candied oranges. Top cakes with candied blood orange slices; serve warm or cool with scoops of ice-cream.

CANDIED BLOOD ORANGES Stir the water, juice and half the sugar in a large frying pan over medium heat until sugar dissolves. Add orange slices; simmer, uncovered, for 20 minutes or until rind is soft. Add remaining sugar to pan; stir gently until dissolved. Simmer, uncovered, a further 10 minutes or until oranges are candied and syrup is thickened slightly. Using a spoon, transfer slices to wire racks on oven trays, in a single layer. Reserve 1 cup (250ml) syrup. Cool. Chop 100g (3 ounces) orange slices for ice-cream.

MASCARPONE ICE-CREAM Bring juice to the boil in a small saucepan; boil for 12 minutes or until reduced to $1/4$ cup (60ml). Cool. Refrigerate until cold. Beat cream, icing sugar and reduced juice in a small bowl with an electric mixer until soft peaks form. Fold in mascarpone and chopped candied orange. Spread mixture level into a 1 litre (4 cup) loaf pan. Cover surface with plastic wrap; freeze for 6 hours or overnight until firm.

TIP Blood oranges are available from late winter through to spring. When buying choose those with the most colour in the skin which is usually an indication that the flesh will be highly coloured too. If unavailable, use 15 regular oranges. Depending on their size you will need 15-18 blood oranges for this recipe.

VARIATION For blood orange hazelnut cakes, use ground hazelnuts instead of almonds in step 4. Serve cakes topped with orange mascarpone instead of the ice-cream: whisk 250g (8 ounces) mascarpone with 1 cup (250ml) pouring cream to soft peaks. Finely chop 100g (3 ounces) of the candied blood oranges and fold into mascarpone mixture.

DO-AHEAD Candied blood orange and ice-cream can be made up to 3 days ahead. The cakes are best made on day of serving.

[PHOTOGRAPH PAGES 68 & 69]

Blood orange cakes with MASCARPONE ICE-CREAM

[RECIPE PAGES 70 & 71]

PREPARING THE BLOOD ORANGES

Use the sharpest knife you have to slice the blood oranges. To assist in evenness, mark out each cut on the rind first, before cutting through the scored line. The slices are cooked first with only half the sugar; this gives the rind a chance to soften before being candied.

DRAINING THE CANDIED BLOOD ORANGES

The candied oranges are ready when syrup has some viscosity or stickiness to it and the oranges are glossy. Remove them from the syrup and place on wire racks over oven trays; leave to cool and dry. You can make candied oranges and lemons in exactly the same way.

MAKING THE MASCARPONE ICE-CREAM

The ice-cream has been devised not to require churning in an ice-cream machine. The fat and sugar content of the ingredients, plus the air incorporated from beating the cream ensure it has a smooth texture. Use a large metal spoon and a lifting and folding action to combine the ingredients.

MAKING THE CAKES

Making the cakes is as simple as combining all the ingredients. To combine ground almonds with other dry ingredients you can sift them together, however this can be tedious. A handy trick is to stir them together with a whisk – this combines the ingredients together and breaks up any lumps at the same time.

BRUSHING CAKES WITH SYRUP

Brush the hot cake with the reserved syrup from the candied oranges. If you are not serving the cakes immediately, you will need to reheat the syrup before serving and brush the hot syrup over cold cakes.

SERVING

Just before serving, top the cakes with the candied blood orange slices and small scoops of ice-cream.

Soft meringue with pineapple and kaffir lime syrup
[RECIPE PAGES 76 & 77]

Soft meringue with pineapple AND KAFFIR LIME SYRUP

PREP + COOK TIME 1 HOUR (+ COOLING) SERVES 6

7 egg whites

1³/₄ cups (375g) caster (superfine) sugar

2 teaspoons cornflour (cornstarch)

2 teaspoons white vinegar

1 small ripe trimmed pineapple (800g), peeled, chopped

2 limes (230g), segmented (see TECHNIQUES)

2 tablespoons small fresh mint leaves

FILLING

250g (8 ounces) mascarpone

¹/₂ cup (125ml) thickened (heavy) cream

1 teaspoons finely grated lime rind

2 teaspoons lime juice

1 tablespoon icing (confectioners') sugar

1 tablespoon finely chopped fresh mint

KAFFIR LIME SYRUP

¹/₂ cup (110g) caster (superfine) sugar

¹/₂ cup (125ml) water

1 fresh stalk lemon grass, trimmed, bruised

6 small kaffir lime leaves

1 Make filling.

2 Make kaffir lime syrup.

3 Preheat oven to 160°C/325°F. Grease a 24cm x 30cm x 3cm (9¹/₂-inch x 12-inch x 1¹/₄-inch) rectangular pan; line base and sides with baking paper.

4 Beat egg whites in a large bowl with an electric mixer until soft peaks form. Gradually add sugar, 1 tablespoon at a time, beating until thick and glossy and sugar has dissolved (about 8 minutes). Fold in cornflour and vinegar. Spoon meringue into pan; smooth the surface, then make furrows lengthways over half the meringue.

5 Bake meringue for 20 minutes, rotating the pan halfway through cooking time, or until meringue is firm to the touch. Stand meringue in pan for 2 minutes before turning out onto a large baking-paper-lined tray dusted with a little icing sugar. Carefully peel away lining paper. Line a second large tray with baking paper, dust with a little more icing sugar. Immediately invert meringue cake onto second lined tray. Cool.

6 Cut meringue in half crossways. Carefully (soft meringue is fragile) place the smooth half on a platter. Spread filling over meringue, top with half of the pineapple and drizzle with a little syrup. Using a wide egg slice or long tart tin base, carefully place remaining meringue on top.

7 Place remaining pineapple in a small bowl with lime segments, mint and a little more syrup; toss to combine. Spoon pineapple mixture on meringue cake; serve drizzled with remaining syrup.

FILLING Beat mascarpone, cream, rind, juice and icing sugar in a small bowl with an electric mixer until soft peaks form; fold in mint. Cover, refrigerate until needed.

KAFFIR LIME SYRUP Place sugar, the water, lemon grass and lime leaves in a small saucepan. Bring to the boil, over medium heat, stirring until sugar dissolves. Simmer for 1 minute.

TIPS Place any leftover lime leaves in a resealable plastic bag and freeze for another use. Add three or four to a curry, scrunching the leaves first to release the flavour; toss thinly sliced leaves through a tropical fruit salad; or add sliced leaves to a jug of iced water for a refreshing citrus flavour. Mango can be substituted for pineapple.

TECHNIQUES Step 7: see *'segmenting citrus'*, page 276.

DO-AHEAD The meringue is best made on day of serving.

[PHOTOGRAPH PAGES 74 & 75]

Lime curd
COCONUT AND
mango cake

PREP + COOK TIME 1 HOUR 15 MINUTES (+ REFRIGERATION) SERVES 8

You will need to start this recipe the day before.

125g (4 ounces) butter
³/₄ cup (165g) caster (superfine) sugar
2 teaspoons finely grated lime rind
2 eggs
90g (3 ounces) white chocolate, melted
1 cup (150g) self-raising flour
¹/₂ cup (70g) macadamias, roasted, chopped finely
¹/₂ cup (40g) desiccated coconut
³/₄ cup (180ml) buttermilk
300ml thickened (heavy) cream
1 tablespoon icing (confectioners') sugar
1 ripe large mango (600g), sliced thinly
2 finger limes, optional (see TIP)

LIME CURD
3 eggs
³/₄ cup (165g) caster (superfine) sugar
¹/₃ cup (80ml) lime juice
150g (4¹/₂ ounces) butter, softened, chopped
2 teaspoons finely grated lime rind

1 Make lime curd.
2 Preheat oven to 180°C/350°F. Grease a 20cm (8-inch) round cake pan; line base and side with baking paper.
3 Beat butter, caster sugar and rind in a medium bowl with an electric mixer until pale and fluffy. Beat in eggs, one at a time, until combined. Fold in chocolate, then flour, nuts, coconut and buttermilk. Spoon mixture into pan; smooth surface.

4 Bake cake for 50 minutes or until a skewer inserted in the centre comes out clean. Stand cake in pan for 5 minutes before turning, top-side up, onto a wire rack to cool.
5 Beat cream and icing sugar in a small bowl with an electric mixer until soft peaks form.
6 Level the top of the cake if necessary; split cake into two layers (see TECHNIQUES). Place the bottom cake layer on a plate; spread with half the lime curd and half the whipped cream. Finish with top cake layer, remaining lime curd and cream. Decorate with mango slices and finger limes.

LIME CURD Whisk eggs, sugar and lime juice in a medium saucepan continuously over low heat for 3 minutes or until thickened to the consistency of custard. Whisk in butter, a small piece at a time, until smooth. Do not boil. Cover surface with plastic wrap; refrigerate for 6 hours or overnight. Stir in rind.

TIP Finger limes are an aromatic native Australian citrus available from selected greengrocers from March to June. Cut in half lengthways to scrape out the juice sacs (vesicles).
TECHNIQUES Step 2: see *'lining a round cake pan'*, page 276. Step 3: see *'melting chocolate'*, page 277. Step 6: see *'levelling a cake'*, page 277 and *'splitting a cake into even layers'*, page 277.
DO-AHEAD The cake, curd, syrup and rind can all be made a day ahead. Store the cake in an airtight container at room temperature; refrigerate curd, syrup and rind separately. Assemble close to serving.

Orange pound cake WITH CANDIED CUMQUATS

PREP + COOK TIME 2 HOURS (+ COOLING) SERVES 6

As the name suggests, pound cakes originally consisted of a pound each of sugar, butter, flour and eggs, which made them very large cakes. These days, any cake that is made with equal proportions of these ingredients takes the name.

1 vanilla bean
170g ($5^{1}/_{2}$ ounces) unsalted butter, softened
$^{3}/_{4}$ cup (165g) caster (superfine) sugar
1 tablespoon finely grated orange rind
3 eggs
1 tablespoon orange juice
1 cup (150g) plain (all-purpose) flour
1 teaspoon baking powder
$1^{1}/_{4}$ cups (300g) fresh soft ricotta
$^{1}/_{2}$ cup (80g) icing (confectioners') sugar
$^{2}/_{3}$ cup (160ml) thick (double) cream (51% butter fat)

CANDIED CUMQUATS

2 cups (325g) cumquats, halved, seeds removed
1 cup (220g) caster (superfine) sugar
$^{3}/_{4}$ cup (180ml) water

1 Make candied cumquats.
2 Preheat oven to 170°C/340°F. Grease two 15cm (6-inch) round cake pans; line base and side with baking paper.
3 Split vanilla bean; scrape seeds (see TECHNIQUES) into a medium bowl of an electric mixer (keep vanilla bean for another use). Add butter, caster sugar and rind to bowl; beat for 5 minutes or until pale and fluffy. Beat in eggs, one at a time,

scraping down the side of the bowl frequently. Add juice and combined sifted flour and baking powder; beat on low speed until just combined. Divide mixture between pans.
4 Bake cakes for 40 minutes or until a skewer inserted into the centre comes out clean. Stand cake in pans for 10 minutes, before turning out onto wire racks to cool.
5 Process ricotta and icing sugar until smooth; transfer to a medium bowl. Beat cream with an electric mixer until soft peaks just form. Fold cream into ricotta mixture.
6 Level top of cakes (see TECHNIQUES); brush each with $^{1}/_{3}$ cup of the cumquat syrup. Place one cake on a cake stand or plate; spread with half the ricotta cream. Finish with second cake and remaining ricotta cream. Decorate with candied cumquats; serve with remaining syrup.

CANDIED CUMQUATS Bring a small saucepan of water to the boil, add cumquats; cook for 1 minute. Drain. Repeat process (this helps to remove any bitterness and soften the rind). Place sugar and the water in a small saucepan over low heat; stir until sugar dissolves. Increase heat to high; bring to the boil. Add cumquats; simmer gently for 30 minutes or until soft and translucent. Cool cumquats in syrup.

TECHNIQUES Step 2: see *'lining a round cake pan'*, page 276.
Step 3: see *'preparing vanilla beans'*, page 276.
Step 6: see *'levelling a cake'*, page 277.
DO-AHEAD The cake and candied cumquats can be made a day ahead. Store cake in an airtight container at room temperature and cumquats in the fridge.

INDULGENT CAKES

Caramel
& NUTS

SMOOTH, BUTTERY

Caramel

and nuts

add gooey

sweetness

AND TEXTURE

Piña colada cake
WITH CARAMEL GLAZE

PREP + COOK TIME 1 HOUR 30 MINUTES (+ STANDING) SERVES 12

The taste of this loose-crumbed pineapple and coconut cake will instantly transport you to the seventies when a piña colada was THE cocktail – albeit without the alcohol hit.

200g (6½ ounces) salted butter, softened
¾ cup (165g) caster (superfine) sugar
2 tablespoons coconut-flavoured liqueur
3 eggs
440g (14 ounces) canned crushed pineapple in natural juice,
    drained well
⅔ cup (160ml) coconut cream
1⅓ cups (105g) desiccated coconut, toasted
1¼ cups (185g) self-raising flour
1 teaspoon baking powder

CARAMEL GLAZE
1½ cups (375ml) thickened (heavy) cream
¾ cup (165g) firmly packed brown sugar
1½ tablespoons liquid glucose syrup (light corn syrup)
½ teaspoon sea salt flakes
1½ teaspoons vanilla extract

1 Preheat oven to 170°C/340°F. Grease a deep 20cm (8-inch) square cake pan; line base and sides with baking paper.

2 Beat butter, sugar and liqueur in a large bowl with an electric mixer until pale and creamy. Beat in eggs, one at a time, until just combined. Fold in pineapple, coconut cream, desiccated coconut and combined sifted flour and baking powder. Spread mixture into pan.

3 Bake cake for 50 minutes or until a skewer inserted into the centre comes out clean. Stand cake in pan for 15 minutes before turning, top-side up, onto a wire rack to cool.

4 Make caramel glaze.

5 Place cake on a wire rack over an oven tray. Pour two-thirds of the glaze over the cake. Stand for 30 minutes or until glaze is cool and set. Serve cake with remaining glaze.

CARAMEL GLAZE Bring cream, sugar, glucose and salt to the boil in small saucepan over low heat, stirring until sugar dissolves. Boil for 20 minutes or until caramel is thick and golden. Remove from heat; stir in extract. Cool for 20 minutes or until thickened.

TIP If the remaining caramel glaze thickens too much by the time of serving, reheat in a small saucepan over low heat, adding 1-2 tablespoons extra cream or water to thin it down.

TECHNIQUES Step 1: see *'lining a square cake pan'*, page 276. Step 4: see also *'making caramel and praline'*, page 277.

DO-AHEAD The cake can be made a day ahead; store in an airtight container at room temperature. The caramel glaze is best made close to serving.

Postre chajá cake
[RECIPE PAGES 90 & 91]

Postre chajá cake

PREP + COOK TIME 1 HOUR 45 MINUTES (+ REFRIGERATION & COOLING) SERVES 8

Postre chajá was created by the owner of a family restaurant in Uruguay. He called his meringue-based dessert 'chajá' after an indigenous bird of the same name, whose abundant white plumage reminded him of the meringue.

395g (12½ ounces) canned sweetened condensed milk
cooking oil spray
6 eggs, separated
½ cup (110g) caster (superfine) sugar
1 teaspoon vanilla extract
2 teaspoons warm water
½ cup (75g) cake flour
¼ cup (35g) cornflour (cornstarch)
¼ teaspoon cream of tartar
300ml thickened (heavy) cream
1 tablespoon icing (confectioners') sugar
120g (4 ounces) bought meringues, crushed coarsely
4 golden kiwifruit (320g), peeled, cut into thin wedges

RUM SYRUP
½ cup (110g) caster (superfine) sugar
½ cup (125ml) water
1½ tablespoons underproof rum

1 Preheat oven to 220°C/425°F.

2 Pour condensed milk into a 1.5-litre (6-cup) ceramic ovenproof dish. Cover dish with foil; crush excess foil upwards. Place ceramic dish in a medium baking dish; add enough boiling water to come halfway up side of the ceramic dish. Bake for 1 hour. Stir mixture; cover, bake a further 30 minutes or until a golden caramel colour, adding extra boiling water to baking dish as needed to maintain water level during baking (see TECHNIQUES). Remove dish from water. Cover; refrigerate for 1 hour, stirring occasionally until mixture is cold.

3 Reduce oven to 160°C/320°F. Using the base of a 20cm (8-inch) round sandwich cake pan as a guide, cut two rounds of baking paper; spray one side of each round with oil. Line two pans with paper, oiled-side down. Do not oil the side of the pans.

4 Beat egg yolks and ⅓ cup (75g) caster sugar in a large bowl with an electric mixer on medium speed for 5 minutes or until thick and pale. Add extract and the water; beat until just incorporated. Sift flours over egg mixture but don't stir in.

5 Beat egg whites in a large bowl of an electric mixer until foamy. Add cream of tartar; beat until soft peaks form. Gradually add remaining caster sugar, beating until firm peaks form.

6 Using a large balloon whisk or metal spoon, gently mix one-third of the egg white mixture into yolk mixture until starting to combine. Mix in remaining egg white mixture until just combined. Divide mixture evenly between pans; spin pans on a work surface to level mixture.

7 Bake cakes for 30 minutes or until a skewer inserted into the centre comes out clean, rotating and swapping cakes on shelves halfway through cooking time. Carefully loosen the sides of cake from pans with a spatula before turning, turn top-side down, onto lightly greased baking-paper-covered wire racks. Cool.

8 Meanwhile, make rum syrup.

9 Level top of cakes; split cakes in half (see TECHNIQUES). Place base of one cake on a cake plate, brush generously with syrup. Using a metal palette knife dipped in hot water, evenly spread one-third of the caramel over cake. Repeat layering twice more with cake, syrup and caramel, finishing with remaining cake.

10 Beat cream and sifted icing sugar in a small bowl with an electric mixer until soft peaks form. Spread cream thickly all over cake. Using cupped hands, press crushed meringue onto top and side of cake. Top cake with kiwifruit. Serve cake immediately or refrigerate, uncovered, for up to 4 hours.

RUM SYRUP Stir sugar and the water in a small heavy-based saucepan over low heat, without simmering, until sugar dissolves. Remove from heat; stir in rum.

TIP For even cake layers, weigh the cake batter and put exactly half into each cake pan.

TECHNIQUES Step 2: see also *'making dulce de leche'*, page 276. Step 9: see *'levelling a cake'*, page 277 and *'splitting a cake into even layers'*, page 277.

DO-AHEAD Cake can be assembled without the cream, meringue and fruit, up to 2 days ahead.

[PHOTOGRAPH PAGES 88 & 89]

Almond, pine nut AND GRAPE CAKE

PREP + COOK TIME **1 HOUR 15 MINUTES (+ STANDING)** SERVES **12**

$1^1/_2$ cup (225g) self-raising flour
$1/_3$ cup (50g) plain (all-purpose) flour
1 cup (120g) ground almonds
$3/_4$ cup (165g) caster (superfine) sugar
$1/_2$ cup (125ml) sweet sherry
4 eggs, beaten lightly
185g (6 ounces) butter, melted
1 tablespoon finely grated lemon rind
1 cup (175g) small seedless red grapes
2 tablespoons pine nuts
125g (4 ounces) marzipan, chopped finely
2 teaspoons icing (confectioners') sugar

SHERRY-FLAVOURED MASCARPONE
250g (8 ounces) mascarpone
2 teaspoons icing (confectioners') sugar
2 tablespoons sweet sherry

1 Preheat oven to 160°C/325°F. Grease a deep 24cm ($9^1/_2$-inch) springform pan; line base and side with baking paper.
2 Sift flours into a large bowl; stir in ground almonds, caster sugar, sherry, eggs, butter and rind. Spread mixture into pan; smooth surface. Scatter with grapes, pine nuts and marzipan.
3 Bake cake for 45 minutes or until a skewer inserted in the centre comes out clean. Stand cake in pan for 15 minutes before transferring to a wire rack to cool slightly.
4 Meanwhile, make sherry-flavoured mascarpone.
5 Dust warm cake with icing sugar and serve with sherry-flavoured mascarpone.

SHERRY-FLAVOURED MASCARPONE Combine ingredients in a small bowl with a wooden spoon.

TIP We used Pedro Ximnez sherry, a dark syrupy style of sherry with a complex taste, however any sweet style is suitable.
TECHNIQUES Step 1: see *'lining a round cake pan'*, page 276.
DO-AHEAD This cake is best made on day of serving.

Pistachio ALMOND CAKE WITH poached persimmons

PREP + COOK TIME **1 HOUR 30 MINUTES (+ COOLING)** SERVES **12**

2 cups (320g) blanched almonds
2 cups (280g) pistachios
2¹/₂ cups (400g) icing (confectioners') sugar
³/₄ teaspoon ground cardamom
2 teaspoons finely grated lemon rind
2 eggs
5 egg whites
green food colouring
¹/₂ cup (40g) flaked almonds
300ml thickened (heavy) cream
¹/₂ cup (140g) Greek-style yoghurt
2 teaspoons icing (confectioners') sugar, extra

POACHED PERSIMMONS
1 vanilla bean
1¹/₂ cups (330g) caster (superfine) sugar
1¹/₂ cups (375ml) water
1 medium lemon (140g), rind peeled thinly
4 persimmons (900g), sliced

1 Preheat oven to 160°C/325°F. Grease a deep 22cm (9-inch) round cake pan; line base with baking paper, line side with three layers of baking paper.
2 Process blanched almonds, pistachios, icing sugar and cardamom until fine; transfer to a large bowl. Stir in rind, eggs and egg whites. Tint green with a few drops of colouring. Spread mixture into pan; smooth surface. Sprinkle evenly with flaked almonds.

3 Bake cake for 1¹/₄ hours; because this cake contains no flour it is tricky to test for doneness using a skewer, instead expect the cake to dome slightly, have a cooked smell and a golden top. Cool cake in pan.
4 Meanwhile, make poached persimmons.
5 Beat cream and yoghurt in a small bowl with an electric mixer until soft peaks form.
6 Place cake on a cake plate or stand; dust with extra sifted icing sugar. Serve with poached persimmons and yoghurt cream.

POACHED PERSIMMONS Split vanilla bean lengthways; scrape seeds (see TECHNIQUES) into a large saucepan, add bean to pan with sugar, the water and rind. Stir over low heat until sugar dissolves; bring to the boil. Reduce heat to a gentle simmer, add persimmons, covering with a round of baking paper; cook for 8 minutes or until just tender. Cool persimmons in syrup.

TIP Covering the persimmons with baking paper while they poach, keeps them submerged in the syrup.
TECHNIQUES Step 1: see *'lining a round cake pan'*, page 276. Step 4: see also *'preparing vanilla beans'*, page 276.
DO-AHEAD The cake and persimmons can be made a day ahead. Store cake in an airtight container at room temperature; store persimmons in an airtight container in the fridge.

Banana
COFFEE AND WALNUT CAKE
with salted caramel frosting

PREP + COOK TIME **3 HOURS (+ REFRIGERATION)** SERVES **12**

395g (12^1/$_2$ ounces) canned sweetened condensed milk

300g (9^1/$_2$ ounces) butter, softened, chopped

^{3}/$_4$ cup (165g) firmly packed brown sugar

2 eggs

1^1/$_2$ cups (225g) self-raising flour

^{1}/$_2$ teaspoon bicarbonate of soda (baking soda)

1 teaspoon ground cinnamon

1^1/$_2$ cups (360g) mashed ripe banana

^{1}/$_2$ cup (120g) sour cream

1 cup (100g) walnut halves, roasted, chopped

3 teaspoons espresso coffee granules

^{1}/$_4$ cup (60ml) boiling water

1 teaspoon sea salt flakes

1 Preheat oven to 220°C/425°F. Grease a deep 20cm (8-inch) round cake pan; line base with baking paper.

2 Pour condensed milk into a 2-litre (8-cup) ceramic ovenproof dish. Cover dish with foil; crush excess foil upwards. Place ceramic dish in a larger baking dish; add enough boiling water into the baking dish to come halfway up side of the ceramic dish. Bake for 1 hour. Stir mixture; cover, bake a further 30 minutes or until mixture is a golden caramel colour, adding extra boiling water to baking dish as needed to maintain water level during baking (see TECHNIQUES). Remove ceramic dish from water. Whisk in 170g (5^1/$_2$ ounces) of the butter, piece by piece, until melted and caramel is smooth. Cover; refrigerate for 1 hour, stirring occasionally until mixture is cold and firm.

3 Reduce oven to 180°C/350°F.

4 Beat remaining butter and the sugar in a small bowl with an electric mixer until pale and fluffy. Beat in eggs, one at a time, until just combined. Transfer mixture to a large bowl. Stir in sifted dry ingredients with mashed banana, sour cream, nuts and combined coffee and water. Spread mixture in pan.

5 Bake cake for 1 hour or until a skewer inserted into the centre comes out clean. Stand cake in pan for 5 minutes before turning, top-side up, onto a wire rack to cool.

6 Beat cold caramel mixture in a small bowl with an electric mixer for 1 minute or until paler and fluffy. Spread caramel frosting on top of cooled cake. Just before serving, sprinkle with salt.

TIP You will need about 4 medium bananas for the amount of mashed banana required.

TECHNIQUES Step 1: see *'lining a round cake pan'*, page 276. Step 2: see also *'making dulce de leche'*, page 276.

DO-AHEAD The cake can be made a day ahead. Store in an airtight container at room temperature in a cool place.

Pecan and spiced apple pull-apart
[RECIPE PAGES 100 & 101]

Pecan and spiced
APPLE PULL-APART

PREP + COOK TIME 1 HOUR (+ REFRIGERATION) SERVES 8

4 medium granny smith apples (600g)

1/4 cup (55g) caster (superfine) sugar

1 tablespoon brown sugar

1 teaspoon ground cinnamon

1/4 teaspoon ground cloves

1 tablespoon water

3 cups (450g) self-raising flour

2 tablespoons caster (superfine) sugar, extra

40g (1 1/2 ounces) cold butter, chopped

1 1/3 cups (330ml) buttermilk

1/2 cup (60g) pecans, roasted, chopped coarsely

1 tablespoon buttermilk, extra

CARAMEL SAUCE

1 cup (220g) firmly packed brown sugar

100g (3 ounces) butter, chopped

300ml pouring cream

TOPPING

1 tablespoon brown sugar

1/2 teaspoon ground cinnamon

1/4 cup (30g) pecans, roasted, chopped coarsely

1 Make caramel sauce, then topping.

2 Preheat oven to 220°C/425°F. Grease a large oven tray; line with baking paper.

3 Peel, core and chop apples into 2cm (3/4-inch) pieces. Place apples in a small saucepan with sugars, spices and the water; stir to combine. Bring to a simmer. Reduce heat to low; cook, covered, for 10 minutes or until apples are tender. Cool. Drain apples; discard liquid.

4 Meanwhile, combine flour and extra caster sugar in a large bowl; rub in butter until mixture resembles crumbs. Add buttermilk; using a dinner knife, cut through mixture mixing to a soft dough. Bring dough together gently on a well-floured surface until no longer sticky.

5 Roll out dough on a well-floured piece of baking paper into a 20cm x 40cm (8-inch x 16-inch) rectangle. Position the dough so a long side is in front of you. Spread apple mixture evenly over dough, leaving a 2cm (³/₄-inch) border on the long side closest to you; scatter with nuts, then drizzle with ¹/₄ cup of the caramel sauce. Using the paper as an aid, roll up dough firmly from the long side; carefully place roll on tray, bringing the two ends together to form a ring. Using a sharp knife, cut eight equally spaced slits into the outside of the ring, towards the centre, cutting three quarters of the way in (see TECHNIQUES). Brush scone ring with buttermilk; sprinkle with topping.
6 Bake ring for 20 minutes, cover loosely with foil halfway through cooking to prevent over browning. Serve scone pull-apart warm, drizzled with warmed caramel sauce.

CARAMEL SAUCE Stir ingredients in a small saucepan over medium heat until sugar dissolves. Simmer for 5 minutes or until thickened slightly.

TOPPING Combine ingredients in a small bowl.

TIP The dough is quite soft so it does need to be handled gently. If you have trouble, or it's a hot day, refrigerate the dough at any stage for about 15 minutes for it to firm-up.
TECHNIQUES Step 5: see also *'cutting cinnamon, apple and pecan pull-apart'*, page 277.
DO-AHEAD The recipe is best made on day of serving.

[PHOTOGRAPH PAGES 98 & 99]

Caramel and peanut butter
MOUSSE MERINGUE CAKE

PREP + COOK TIME 1 HOUR 40 MINUTES (+ COOLING & REFRIGERATION) SERVES 8

3 egg whites
1 cup (160g) icing (confectioners') sugar
3 teaspoons cornflour (cornstarch)
³/₄ cup (100g) ground almonds
4 teaspoons powdered gelatine
2 tablespoons cold water
¹/₂ cup (140g) smooth peanut butter
¹/₂ cup (170g) canned caramel top 'n' fill
1 cup (250ml) thickened (heavy) cream
1¹/₂ cups (375ml) thick (double) cream
1 tablespoon dutch-processed cocoa

PEANUT CARAMEL SAUCE
¹/₂ cup (110g) caster (superfine) sugar
2 tablespoons water
1 cup (250ml) thickened (heavy) cream
¹/₃ cup (70g) smooth peanut butter
¹/₃ cup (45g) coarsely chopped roasted peanuts

1 Preheat oven to 160°C/325°F. Lock the base in two 22cm (9-inch) springform pans upside down; grease, then line the base and side with baking paper.

2 Beat egg whites in a small bowl with an electric mixer until soft peaks form. Gradually add sifted icing sugar, beating until thick and glossy. Beat in cornflour and ground almonds until well combined. Divide mixture between pans; smooth surface with a palette knife.

3 Bake meringues for 40 minutes, swapping pans from top to bottom halfway through cooking time, or until crisp and dry. Cool in oven with door ajar.

4 Meanwhile, make peanut caramel sauce.

5 To make mousse, sprinkle gelatine over the water in a small bowl; stand for 5 minutes (see TECHNIQUES). Whisk peanut butter, caramel top 'n' fill and thickened cream in a small saucepan over low heat until well combined. Increase heat to medium; bring to the boil. Remove from heat; stir in gelatine mixture until dissolved. Transfer to a medium bowl; cool. Whisk thick cream just until soft peaks form; fold into peanut butter mixture.

6 Spoon mousse on one meringue in pan. Remove second meringue from pan; place on top of mousse. Refrigerate for 2 hours or until set.

7 Before serving, dust cake with cocoa. Serve topped with peanut caramel sauce.

PEANUT CARAMEL SAUCE Stir sugar and the water in a small saucepan over medium heat, without boiling, until sugar dissolves. Cook for 10 minutes without stirring or until a golden brown caramel. Remove from heat. Taking care as the mixture will splutter, add cream. Return pan heat; stir until smooth then stir in peanut butter and peanuts. Cool. (See TECHNIQUES.)

TECHNIQUES Step 1: see *'lining a round cake pan'*, page 276.
Step 4: see also *'making caramel and praline'*, page 277.
Step 5: see also *'dissolving gelatine powder'*, page 277.
DO-AHEAD The meringue layers can be made up to 3 days ahead; store in an air-tight container at room temperature.

Banoffee meringue with honeycomb
[RECIPE PAGES 106 & 107]

Banoffee meringue
WITH HONEYCOMB

PREP + COOK TIME **3 HOURS (+ COOLING)** SERVES **12**

4 egg whites

$^1/_4$ teaspoon cream of tartar

$^1/_4$ cup (55g) caster (superfine) sugar

$^3/_4$ cup (165g) firmly packed brown sugar

2 teaspoons cornflour (cornstarch)

1 teaspoon white vinegar

$^1/_4$ teaspoon vanilla extract

2 medium bananas (400g), sliced

1 tablespoon caster (superfine) sugar, extra

300ml thick (double) cream (56% butter fat)

100g (3 ounces) honeycomb, chopped coarsely

DULCE DE LECHE

395g (12$^1/_2$ ounces) canned sweetened condensed milk

1 Make dulce de leche.

2 Preheat oven to 120°C/250°F. Line two large oven trays with baking paper. Mark two 12.5cm x 30cm (5-inch x 12-inch) rectangles on paper; turn, marked-side down, on trays.

3 Beat egg whites, cream of tartar and sugars in a medium bowl with an electric mixer on high speed for 8 minutes or until thick and glossy and sugar is dissolved. Beat in cornflour, vinegar and extract on low speed. Divide mixture evenly between trays, spreading to cover just inside marked rectangles; swirl meringue.

4 Bake meringue for 1 hour or until dry to touch. Cool in oven with door ajar.

5 Place banana slices, in a single layer, on an oven tray; sprinkle with extra caster sugar. Using a blowtorch, caramelise sugar.

6 Whisk dulce de leche in a medium bowl until smooth. Whisk cream in a small bowl until soft peaks form.

7 Place one meringue on a platter. Spread two-thirds of the cream on meringue. Drop spoonfuls of half the dulce de leche on cream. Repeat layering with remaining meringue, cream and dulce de leche. Top with banana slices and honeycomb.

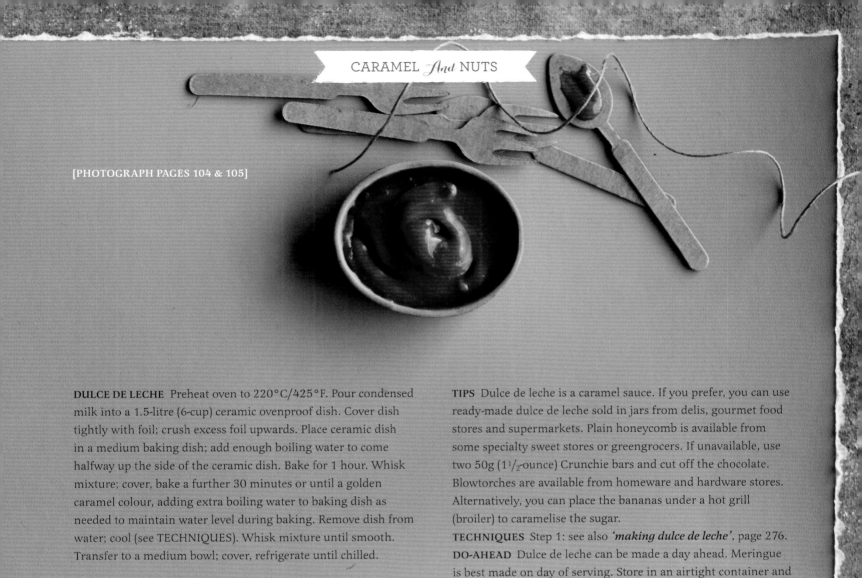

[PHOTOGRAPH PAGES 104 & 105]

DULCE DE LECHE Preheat oven to 220°C/425°F. Pour condensed milk into a 1.5-litre (6-cup) ceramic ovenproof dish. Cover dish tightly with foil; crush excess foil upwards. Place ceramic dish in a medium baking dish; add enough boiling water to come halfway up the side of the ceramic dish. Bake for 1 hour. Whisk mixture; cover, bake a further 30 minutes or until a golden caramel colour, adding extra boiling water to baking dish as needed to maintain water level during baking. Remove dish from water; cool (see TECHNIQUES). Whisk mixture until smooth. Transfer to a medium bowl; cover, refrigerate until chilled.

TIPS Dulce de leche is a caramel sauce. If you prefer, you can use ready-made dulce de leche sold in jars from delis, gourmet food stores and supermarkets. Plain honeycomb is available from some specialty sweet stores or greengrocers. If unavailable, use two 50g (1½-ounce) Crunchie bars and cut off the chocolate. Blowtorches are available from homeware and hardware stores. Alternatively, you can place the bananas under a hot grill (broiler) to caramelise the sugar.

TECHNIQUES Step 1: see also *'making dulce de leche'*, page 276.

DO-AHEAD Dulce de leche can be made a day ahead. Meringue is best made on day of serving. Store in an airtight container and assemble close to serving.

Banoffee meringue WITH HONEYCOMB

[RECIPE PAGES 106 & 107]

BEATING THE MERINGUE

If using hand held beaters for the meringue, steady the bowl on a tea towel and ensure that you move the beaters around the bowl for even beating. For best results, use a deep, small bowl as this allows the beaters to beat volume into the the egg whites. The meringue is ready when it's glossy and forms stiff peaks.

SPREADING THE MERINGUE

To achieve the lovely rounded edge of our meringue, place spoonfuls of meringue close together just inside traced rectangle, then fill the centre with random spoonfuls. Spread the mixture evenly, from the outside in, trying to avoid touching the outer edge.

CARAMELISING THE BANANAS

Hold the blowtorch 10cm (4-inches) above the bananas. Adjust the flame so the inner darker portion of the flame almost touches the sugar; move it in slow sweeping movements. As the sugar heats it will dissolve and finally caramelise. Don't be afraid to add extra sugar if necessary to achieve this.

LAYERING WITH CREAM

Assemble the meringue only when you are ready to serve. Spread cream using an offset spatula or the back of dessert spoon, leaving a border of meringue; top with the dulce de leche, then another meringue layer.

SPOONING THE DULCE DE LECHE

Top the second meringue layer with the remaining cream then drizzle over the remaining dulce de leche, before finishing with banana slices and honeycomb.

SERVING

The luscious multi-textured layers of this cake mean it will be a little bit messy to serve but don't worry. Cut the cake using a finely serrated knife and place on plates, or for a modern approach serve in glasses.

STORING NUTS

Nuts are high in oils, which makes them prone to rancidity, store in airtight containers in the freezer to prevent it.

Roasting nuts

ROASTING ACCENTUATES THE FLAVOUR OF NUTS AND HIDES ANY STALENESS. WITH THE EXCEPTION OF PINE NUTS, IT IS BETTER TO ROAST THEM IN THE OVEN AS OPPOSED TO THE STOVE TOP, AS IT'S HARDER TO HEAT THE NUTS THROUGH SUFFICIENTLY WITHOUT SCORCHING THE EXTERIOR FIRST. MOST NUTS WILL TAKE 8 MINUTES IN A 180°C/350°F OVEN.

BUYING NUTS Buy nuts from places with a high turnover. While supermarkets do have high turnover, long warehouse storage can lessen this advantage. Seek out Greek and Middle Eastern stores as these cultures use a lot of nuts and therefore have an appreciation for freshness, as do health food stores.

Nut SUBSTITUTES

Feel free to play around with nuts other than those we've suggested in our recipes. As long as your chosen nut substitute equals the weight of the original quantity you will be fine.

MAKING GROUND ALMONDS

You can make your own ground almonds from either blanched or almond kernels. The flavour will be slightly more superior if you use kernels. Use a coffee grinder to do this in small batches. You can do the same with hazelnuts.

ACHIEVING THE PERFECT COLOUR TRICKS

Once the caramel starts to colour, swirl the pan gently to ensure it does so evenly, but don't stir. As it colours it will do so quickly and will continue to do so off the heat. If you are new to making caramel, it's better to remove it from the heat a little earlier and wait for it to continue to deepen off the heat.

Perfect Caramel

The single most important thing when make a water-sugar based caramel is to ensure that all sugar crystals dissolve to prevent crystallisation. To guarantee this, dissolve the sugar before the mixture boils; dip a pastry brush in cold water and brush down the side of the pan to remove any undissolved sugar crystals. Adding a teaspoon of lemon juice at the start also discourages crystallisation.

HOW DARK SHOULD CARAMEL BE? As a caramel darkens it takes on more flavour. If a caramel is too light it will simply taste sweet, too dark and it will be bitter. A mid-golden caramel is ideal as it will offer less sweetness and more caramel taste.

Taking CARE

Take great care when making caramel as it reaches a high temperature. If a cool liquid is to be added to a caramel it will splatter, so stand back and add it gradually. Remember that if you pour caramel into a metal pan, the pan itself will become hot so use oven mitts. Should you burn yourself, place the injured skin under cold running water for several minutes before seeking first aid.

HOW DO I STOP MY CARAMEL COOKING?

IF YOUR CARAMEL IS THE PERFECT COLOUR ON THE HEAT, THE CHANCES ARE IT HAS GONE TOO FAR AS IT WILL CONTINUE TO DARKEN. TO STOP IT, PLACE THE SAUCEPAN IN A SINK WITH ENOUGH COLD WATER TO COME ONE-THIRD OF THE WAY UP THE SIDE OF THE PAN TO COOL IT RAPIDLY.

Hazelnut choc chip cake with
FRANGELICO CREAM AND FIGS

PREP + COOK TIME **1 HOUR 45 MINUTES (+ COOLING)** SERVES **12**

1 cup (140g) skinless roasted hazelnuts

1 tablespoon icing (confectioners') sugar

4 egg whites

1 cup (220g) caster (superfine) sugar

100g (3 ounces) dark (semi-sweet) chocolate, chopped

100g (3 ounces) hazelnut wafer biscuits, quartered

4 medium figs (240g), cut into wedges

2 tablespoons brown sugar

FRANGELICO CREAM

250g (8 ounces) crème fraîche

$^1/_2$ cup (125ml) thick (double) cream (48% butter fat)

$^1/_4$ cup (40g) icing (confectioners') sugar

$^1/_3$ cup (80ml) Frangelico liqueur

1 Preheat oven to 160°C/325°F. Lock the base in a 22cm (9-inch) springform pan upside down; grease, then line base and side with baking paper.

2 Rinse nuts under cold water; drain well. Spread nuts on a baking-paper-lined oven tray; dust with sifted icing sugar, toss to coat. Roast for 8 minutes or until lightly browned. Reserve $^1/_4$ cup for decoration. Chop remaining nuts; cool.

3 Beat egg whites and $^1/_4$ cup (55g) caster sugar in a small bowl with an electric mixer on high speed until firm peaks form. Add remaining caster sugar; beat on high speed for 8 minutes or until dissolved. Transfer mixture to a large bowl; fold in chopped nuts, chocolate and wafer biscuits. Spoon mixture into pan.

4 Bake cake for 40 minutes or until firm. Cool in pan.

5 Make frangelico cream.

6 Remove cake from pan; transfer to a plate. Gently press down top of meringue; spread with frangelico cream.

7 Place figs, in a single layer, on a shallow oven tray; sprinkle with brown sugar. Using a blowtorch, brown the figs until sugar caramelises.

8 Arrange figs on cake and drizzle with any cooking juices. Sprinkle with reserved nuts.

FRANGELICO CREAM Beat ingredients in a small bowl with an electric mixer until soft peaks form.

TIPS While we used Frangelico in this recipe, you can use your favourite hazelnut-flavoured liqueur. Locking in the base of a springform pan upside down, makes it easier to remove the cake later. Blowtorches are available from kitchenware and hardware stores. Alternatively, you can place the tray of figs under a hot grill (broiler) to caramelise the sugar.

TECHNIQUES Step 1: see *'lining a round cake pan'*, page 276.

DO-AHEAD The cake can be made a day ahead; store in an airtight container at room temperature. Fill and decorate just before serving.

Amaretto and caramel ICE-CREAM CAKE

PREP + COOK TIME 50 MINUTES (+ CHURNING & FREEZING) SERVES 12

You will need an ice-cream machine and you'll need to start this recipe the day before.

3 cups (750ml) milk
3 cups (750ml) pouring cream
18 egg yolks
2 cups (440g) caster (superfine) sugar
2¹/₂ tablespoons amaretto
220g (7 ounces) amaretti biscuits, crushed roughly
1 tablespoon amaretto, extra

CARAMEL SAUCE
2 cups (440g) caster (superfine) sugar
¹/₂ cup (125ml) water
1¹/₂ tablespoons liquid glucose
1 cup (250ml) pouring cream
120g (4 ounces) butter, softened, chopped

1 Heat milk and cream in a large saucepan until almost boiling. Whisk egg yolks and sugar in a large bowl until combined. Gradually whisk milk mixture into yolk mixture. Return mixture to pan; stir constantly over low heat for 7 minutes or until custard thickens. Do not boil. Strain mixture into a large bowl; stir in liqueur. Cover surface with plastic wrap; refrigerate 4 hours or until chilled.
2 Meanwhile, make caramel sauce.
3 Grease a 22cm (9-inch) springform pan; line base and side with baking paper. Reserve 1 tablespoon amaretti crumbs to serve. Sprinkle one-third of the remaining amaretti crumbs on base of the pan. Place pan in freezer to chill.
4 Churn half the chilled custard in an ice-cream machine according to manufacturer's instructions. Working quickly, spoon ice-cream into chilled pan; smooth surface. Using a quarter of the caramel sauce, dollop four tablespoons onto the ice-cream layer. Using a knife, gently swirl the caramel through ice-cream. Sprinkle with half the remaining amaretti crumbs. Cover with plastic wrap; freeze for 1 hour or until firm.
5 Repeat step 4 with remaining chilled custard, another quarter of the caramel sauce and remaining amaretti crumbs. Cover with plastic wrap; freeze overnight until firm. Stir extra amaretto into caramel sauce; refrigerate until required.
6 Before serving, reheat remaining caramel sauce in a microwave oven on low. Drizzle sauce over ice-cream cake; sprinkle with reserved amaretti.

CARAMEL SAUCE Stir sugar and the water in a medium saucepan over medium heat until sugar dissolves, brushing down side of pan occasionally with a wet pastry brush. Bring to the boil. Reduce heat; simmer, without stirring, for 7 minutes or until a deep caramel colour (see TECHNIQUES). Remove pan from heat. Carefully add cream, taking care as mixture will splutter. Return to heat; stir until smooth. Cool caramel until just warm. Gradually whisk in butter until combined. Transfer sauce to a jug, cover; set aside at room temperature until required.

TIP This recipe only uses egg yolks, which of course means you will have 18 egg whites left over. The good news is that you can freeze them for later use. As you separate the eggs, place each white into the hole of an ice-cube tray. Once frozen transfer them to a small container or resealable plastic bag, and note the date; they will keep for up to 1 year. Thaw in the fridge before use.
TECHNIQUES Step 2: see *'making caramel and praline'*, page 277. Step 3: see *'lining a round cake pan'*, page 276.

Triple-caramel mud cake

PREP + COOK TIME **5 HOURS 30 MINUTES (+ REFRIGERATION & STANDING)** SERVES **16**

395g (12¹/₂ ounces) canned sweetened condensed milk
250g (8 ounces) unsalted butter, chopped
1 cup (220g) firmly packed dark brown sugar
¹/₄ teaspoon sea salt flakes
¹/₄ cup (60ml) butterscotch schnapps
1¹/₂ cups (225g) plain (all-purpose) flour
¹/₂ cup (75g) self-raising flour
2 eggs

CARAMELISED WHITE CHOCOLATE GANACHE
300g (9¹/₂ ounces) white chocolate, chopped finely
¹/₂ cup (125ml) pouring cream

1 Make caramelised white chocolate ganache.
2 Preheat oven to 220°C/425°F.
3 Pour condensed milk into a 2-litre (8-cup) ceramic ovenproof dish. Cover dish with foil; crush excess foil upwards. Place ceramic dish in a larger baking dish; add enough boiling water to come halfway up side of the ceramic dish. Bake for 1 hour. Stir mixture; cover, bake a further 30 minutes or until a golden caramel colour, adding extra boiling water to baking dish as needed to maintain water level during baking (see TECHNIQUES). Whisk caramel until smooth. Cover; cool to room temperature.
4 Reduce oven to 160°C/325°F. Grease a deep 20cm (8-inch) round cake pan; line base and side with baking paper.
5 Stir butter, sugar and salt in a medium saucepan over low heat, without boiling, until smooth. Add caramel and schnapps; whisk until smooth. Transfer mixture to a large bowl; cool for 15 minutes. Whisk in sifted flours, then eggs; pour into pan.

6 Bake cake for 1 hour. Cover pan loosely with foil; bake another 1 hour or until a skewer inserted into the centre comes out clean. Stand cake in pan for 15 minutes before turning, top-side up, onto a wire rack to cool.
7 Place cake on a plate; spread top with ganache.

CARAMELISED WHITE CHOCOLATE GANACHE Preheat oven to 160°C/325°F. Scatter chocolate evenly over base of a shallow baking dish; bake for 20 minutes, stirring twice or until caramel in colour. Transfer to a large bowl. Bring cream almost to the boil in a small saucepan; whisk in chocolate until almost smooth. Strain mixture through a fine sieve, pushing down on solids; discard solids. Cover; refrigerate for 30 minutes, stirring occasionally, or until ganache is of a spreadable consistency.

TIP Butterscotch schnapps is available from liquor stores and adds quite a significant butterscotch flavour to this cake. Although it has a slightly different flavour, you can use irish cream instead.
TECHNIQUES Step 3: see also *'making dulce de leche'*, page 276. Step 4: see *'lining a round cake pan'*, page 276.
DO-AHEAD The caramel and caramelised white chocolate ganache can be made a day ahead; store in an airtight+ container in the fridge. Bring to room temperature before assembling cake.

Pecan, fig and MAPLE MASCARPONE CAKE

PREP + COOK TIME 1 HOUR 30 MINUTES SERVES 10

1¼ cups (150g) pecans
¾ cup (110g) self-raising flour
½ cup (75g) plain (all-purpose) flour
250g (8 ounces) butter, softened
½ cup (110g) caster (superfine) sugar
½ cup (160g) fig jam
3 eggs
4 medium figs (120g), halved

PECAN PRALINE
½ cup (110g) caster (superfine) sugar
½ cup (125ml) water
½ cup (60g) pecans, roasted

MAPLE MASCARPONE CREAM
300ml thickened (heavy) cream
250g (8 ounces) mascarpone
2 tablespoons maple syrup
½ cup (80g) icing (confectioners') sugar

1 Preheat oven to 170°C/340°F. Grease a deep 22cm (9-inch) round cake pan; line base and side with baking paper, extending the paper 5cm (2 inches) above side.
2 Process nuts and flours until nuts are finely ground. Beat butter, sugar and jam in a small bowl with an electric mixer until pale and fluffy. Beat in eggs, one at a time. Transfer mixture to a large bowl; stir in flour mixture. Spread mixture into pan.

3 Bake cake for 55 minutes or until a skewer inserted into the centre comes out clean. Stand cake in pan 5 minutes before turning, top-side up, onto a wire rack to cool.
4 Meanwhile, make pecan praline, then maple mascarpone cream.
5 Split cold cake into three layers (see TECHNIQUES). Spread bottom cake layer with one-third of mascarpone cream. Top with middle cake layer; spread with one-third of mascarpone cream. Finish with top cake layer and remaining mascarpone cream. Decorate with figs and coarsely chopped praline.

PECAN PRALINE Stir sugar and the water in a small saucepan over low heat, without boiling, until sugar dissolves. Bring to the boil; boil, without stirring, for 10 minutes or until a golden caramel. Add nuts; swirl to coat in caramel. Pour onto a baking-paper-lined oven tray. Stand at room temperature until set. (See TECHNIQUES.)

MAPLE MASCARPONE CREAM Beat ingredients in a small bowl with an electric mixer until firm peaks form.

TECHNIQUES Step 1: see *'lining a round cake pan'*, page 276. Step 4: see also *'making caramel and praline'*, page 277. Step 5: see also *'splitting a cake into even layers'*, page 277.
DO-AHEAD The cake and praline can be made a day ahead; store in separate airtight containers at room temperature. Chop praline and decorate cake just before serving.

Pecan, fig and
MAPLE MASCARPONE CAKE

[RECIPE PAGE 119]

ADDING FLOUR TO THE CREAMED MIXTURE

Using a wooden spoon, stir in the flour just until combined. Don't stir too briskly, or for too long, or you will toughen the cake.

MAKING THE PECAN PRALINE

Make sure you line the tray with baking paper before you make the caramel, as once the caramel is golden you will need to work quickly. For more information on making praline see '*making caramel and praline*', page 277.

MAKING THE MASCARPONE CREAM

Place all ingredients in a bowl and beat to stiff peaks, taking care not to overbeat the mixture. Because of the high butter fat content of the ingredients this will happen quickly.

SPLITTING THE CAKE INTO LAYERS

Hold the knife horizontal to the cake to cut layers. For more details *'splitting cakes into even layers'*, see page 277. If the cake is crumbly, use a pastry brush to remove loose crumbs so they aren't combined with the cream.

LAYERING THE CAKE

Using a metal palette knife or offset spatula held in a horizontal position, spread the mascarpone in even layers, with sweeping movements. Because the mixture is quite thick, you can take it almost to the edge of the cake. Rotate the cake stand or plate as you spread, checking that the filling is level.

SERVING

Break the praline into pieces with your hands, then chop them into finer pieces with a knife. The figs look prettier torn rather than cut. To do this, make a small cut in the base of the fig, then pull apart in halves from the cut using your thumbs. Place on the top of the cake with the praline.

INDULGENT CAKES

Berries
& CREAM

FLORAL, PERFUMED

Berries

and cream

signal the arrival of

summer

IN ABUNDANCE

Chocolate cherry
BERRY PAVLOVA

PREP + COOK TIME 2 HOURS (+ COOLING) SERVES 10

100g (3 ounces) dark chocolate (70% cocoa), chopped
4 egg whites
1 cup (220g) caster (superfine) sugar
1 tablespoon cornflour (cornstarch)
1 teaspoon white vinegar
250g (8 ounces) cream cheese, softened
2 teaspoons vanilla extract
1/4 cup (40g) icing (confectioners') sugar
300ml thickened (heavy) cream
fresh cherries with stems attached

CHERRY BLUEBERRY COMPOTE
2 cups (300g) cherries, halved, pitted
1 cup (150g) blueberries
1/3 cup (75g) caster (superfine) sugar
1/4 cup (60ml) water
1/4 cup (80g) cherry jam

1 Preheat oven to 120°C/250°F. Line an oven tray with baking paper. Mark an 18cm (7 1/4-inch) circle on paper.
2 Place chocolate in a small heatproof bowl over a small saucepan of simmering water (don't allow bowl to touch water); stir until just melted (see TECHNIQUES). Cool slightly.
3 Beat egg whites in a small bowl with an electric mixer until soft peaks form; gradually add caster sugar, beating until dissolved after each addition, and mixture is thick and glossy.

4 Fold cornflour and vinegar into meringue mixture; swirl in chocolate. Dollop meringue inside marked circle on tray.
5 Bake meringue for 1 1/4 hours or until dry to the touch. Turn oven off, leave meringue to cool in oven with door ajar.
6 Meanwhile, make cherry blueberry compote.
7 Beat cream cheese, extract and icing sugar in a small bowl with an electric mixer until smooth; gradually beat in cream until smooth and combined.
8 Just before serving, spoon cream cheese mixture on pavlova; top with compote. Decorate with fresh cherries.

CHERRY BLUEBERRY COMPOTE Place cherries, blueberries, sugar and the water in a medium saucepan over medium heat; bring to a simmer. Simmer for 5 minutes or until cherries and blueberries have released juices. Using a slotted spoon, transfer cherries and blueberries to a small bowl. Stir jam into juices in pan; bring to the boil. Boil for 5 minutes or until mixture thickens. Pour syrup over cherry mixture. Cool completely.

TIP To check that you have beaten the meringue sufficiently, rub a little of the mixture between your fingers – it should feel silky smooth, without any grainy sugar crystals.
TECHNIQUES Step 2: see also *'melting chocolate'*, page 277.
DO-AHEAD The pavlova can be made a day ahead; store in an airtight container at room temperature. Topping is best made close to serving.

Berry and tamarillo croissant pudding cake
[RECIPE PAGES 130 & 131]

Berry and tamarillo
CROISSANT PUDDING CAKE

PREP + COOK TIME 2 HOURS (+ REFRIGERATION & COOLING) SERVES 12

8 croissants (400g), each torn into 4 pieces

125g (4 ounces) raspberries

600ml pouring cream

1 cup (250ml) milk

2/3 cup (150g) caster (superfine) sugar

8 eggs

1 teaspoon vanilla bean paste

2 tablespoons demerara sugar

BERRY AND TAMARILLO JAM

5 tamarillos (660g)

250g (8 ounces) strawberries, halved (quartered if large)

1 cup (220g) caster (superfine) sugar

1 tablespoon finely grated tangelo rind

1/2 teaspoon vanilla bean paste

1 star anise

1 Make berry and tamarillo jam.

2 Preheat oven to 160°C/325°F. Line base and side of a 24cm (9½-inch) springform pan with one piece of extra wide foil, taking care not to tear foil. Line base only with baking paper; grease whole pan well.

3 Place croissant pieces, torn-side up, in pan; spoon three-quarters of the jam on croissants. Cut reserved tamarillo into thin wedges; place two-thirds of the slices between croissant pieces. Top with raspberries.

4 Add remaining tamarillo wedges to jam; stir to combine. Refrigerate until needed.

5 Whisk cream, milk, caster sugar, eggs and paste in a large bowl until combined. Slowly pour custard over croissant and fruit; gently shake pan to ensure custard is evenly distributed.

6 Place pan on an oven tray; bake for 1½ hours or until golden and just set (custard should still wobble as it will set further on standing). Sprinkle with demerara sugar; stand in pan for 30 minutes. Serve pudding cake warm or at room temperature, topped with remaining jam and, if you like, whipped cream.

BERRY AND TAMARILLO JAM Score skin at the base of each tamarillo with a sharp knife; plunge into boiling water briefly then into iced water. Remove skin; reserve 3 tamarillos for pudding. Chop each remaining tamarillo into 12 pieces; place in a small heavy-based saucepan. Add strawberries, sugar, rind, paste and star anise; cook, covered, over low heat, shaking pan occasionally for 5 minutes. Simmer, uncovered, a further 15 minutes or until mixture thickens. Strain mixture through a fine sieve over a heatproof bowl. Return syrup to pan; simmer over medium heat until reduced by half. Combine reduced syrup with fruit; cool.

TIP Lining the cake pan with a layer of foil will keep it 'water tight' during cooking.

DO-AHEAD The jam can be made a day ahead. Store in an airtight container in the fridge. The pudding is best made on the day.

[PHOTOGRAPH PAGES 128 & 129]

Berry and coconut
TRES LECHES CAKE

PREP + COOK TIME 1 HOUR 20 MINUTES (+ COOLING) SERVES 9

This delicious Latin American sponge cake soaked in three milks (tres leche) is perfect for those who like their cakes on the sweet side.

250g (8 ounces) strawberries
125g (4 ounces) blueberries
125g (4 ounces) raspberries
4 eggs, separated
1 cup (220g) caster (superfine) sugar
$1/_3$ cup (80ml) milk
1 teaspoon vanilla extract
$1^1/_3$ cups (200g) plain (all-purpose) flour
1 teaspoon baking powder
395g ($12^1/_2$ ounce) canned sweetened condensed milk
$1/_2$ cup (125ml) evaporated milk
$1/_2$ cup (125ml) coconut cream

WHIPPED COCONUT CREAM
$1/_4$ cup (60ml) coconut cream, chilled
300ml thickened (heavy) cream, chilled
2 tablespoons icing (confectioners') sugar
$1/_2$ teaspoon vanilla extract

1 Preheat oven to 160°C/325°F. Grease a 22cm (9-inch) square cake pan; line base and sides with baking paper, extending the paper 5cm (2-inches) above top.
2 Place half of all the berries in a bowl; refrigerate until ready to serve. Chop remaining strawberries, then combine with remaining blueberries and remaining raspberries.

3 Beat egg whites in a medium bowl with an electric mixer until soft peaks form. Gradually add sugar, beating until glossy and stiff. Combine egg yolks, milk and extract in a small bowl. With the motor operating, gradually add milk mixture to the egg white mixture, beating until well combined. Sift flour and baking powder onto mixture, then gently fold through; fold in berries. Pour mixture into pan; level surface.
4 Bake cake for 1 hour, turning pan halfway through cooking, or until a skewer inserted into the centre comes out clean.
5 Meanwhile, whisk condensed milk, evaporated milk and coconut cream together in a large jug until combined.
6 As soon as the cake is cooked, use a skewer to poke holes in the cake; pour milk mixture over hot cake. Cool cake in pan.
7 Meanwhile, make whipped coconut cream.
8 Spread whipped coconut cream on cake; decorate with reserved berries.

WHIPPED COCONUT CREAM Push coconut cream through a fine sieve into a small bowl. Beat thickened cream, sifted icing sugar and extract in a small bowl with an electric mixer until almost soft peaks form. Fold in sieved coconut cream.

TIPS Shake the can of coconut cream before you open it. You can use whatever berries you like, such as mulberries and loganberries. The cake is easier to cut using a flat-bladed knife, rather than serrated.
TECHNIQUES Step 1: see *'lining a square cake pan'*, page 276.
DO-AHEAD This cake is best made on day of serving.

Lemon ricotta semolina cake with cherry syrup
[RECIPE PAGES 136 & 137]

Lemon ricotta semolina cake
WITH CHERRY SYRUP

PREP + COOK TIME 1 HOUR 20 MINUTES (+ COOLING) SERVES 8

250g (8 ounces) butter, softened

1¼ cups (275g) caster (superfine) sugar

1 tablespoon finely grated lemon rind

3 eggs

1 cup (250g) smooth packaged ricotta

⅓ cup (80ml) lemon juice

1 cup (150g) self-raising flour

1 cup (160g) fine semolina

CHERRY SYRUP

2 teaspoons cornflour (cornstarch)

1 cup (250ml) cold tap water

1 cup (220g) caster (superfine) sugar

2 tablespoons brandy

5cm (2-inch) strip lemon rind

2 tablespoons lemon juice

500g (1 pound) cherries

CHERRY BRANDY CREAM

300ml thickened (heavy) cream

1 tablespoon brandy

1 Preheat oven to 180°C/350°F. Grease a deep 21cm (8½-inch) bundt pan well (see tips); dust with flour, shake out excess.

2 Beat butter, sugar and rind in a small bowl with an electric mixer until pale and fluffy. Beat in eggs, one at a time. Transfer mixture to a large bowl; stir in ricotta, juice, sifted flour and semolina. Spoon mixture into pan.

3 Bake cake for 45 minutes or until a skewer inserted into the centre comes out clean. Stand cake in pan for 5 minutes before turning out onto a wire rack to cool.

4 Meanwhile, make cherry syrup, then cherry brandy cream.

5 Serve warm cake drizzled with warm syrup and cream.

CHERRY SYRUP Blend cornflour and the water in a medium saucepan until smooth. Add sugar, brandy, rind and juice; stir over medium-low heat, without boiling, until sugar dissolves. Bring to the boil. Add cherries; simmer, uncovered, 10 minutes or until cherries are tender and syrup thickens. Cool. Reserve 2 tablespoons cooled syrup for cherry brandy cream.

CHERRY BRANDY CREAM Beat cream, reserved cooled syrup and brandy in a small bowl with an electric mixer until soft peaks form.

TIPS It is important to grease a bundt pan really well with butter, making sure you cover all edges and corners. Make sure you use the packaged variety of ricotta in this recipe, as it has a cream-like consistency, rather than the deli ricotta, portioned from a round, which is drier.

VARIATION For a ricotta orange and semolina cake with sticky strawberries: substitute orange rind and juice for the lemon rind and juice in step 2. For a sticky strawberry syrup, use 500g (1 pound) strawberries instead of the cherries and reduce the simmering time to 5 minutes.

DO-AHEAD The cake and syrup can be made a day ahead; refrigerate, separately, in airtight containers. Reheat the cake and syrup before serving.

[PHOTOGRAPH PAGES 134 & 135]

Strawberries and cream
WHITE CHOCOLATE ROULADE

PREP + COOK TIME 45 MINUTES (+ STANDING & REFRIGERATION) SERVES 10

5 eggs, separated

$^2/_3$ cup (150g) caster (superfine) sugar

1$^1/_2$ tablespoons hot water

80g (2$^1/_2$ ounces) white chocolate, grated finely

$^2/_3$ cup (100g) self-raising flour

$^1/_4$ cup (55g) caster (superfine) sugar, extra

375g (12 ounces) strawberries, sliced thinly

2 tablespoons icing (confectioners') sugar

$^1/_2$ teaspoon sumac

250g (8 ounces) mascarpone

$^1/_2$ cup (125ml) thickened (heavy) cream

30g (1 ounce) store-bought meringue nests, crushed coarsely

1 Preheat oven to 200°C/400°F. Grease a 26cm x 32cm (10$^1/_2$-inch x 12$^3/_4$-inch) swiss roll pan; line base and long sides with baking paper, extending the paper 5cm (2 inches) over edge.

2 Beat egg yolks and caster sugar in a medium bowl with an electric mixer for 5 minutes or until very thick and pale. Pour the hot water down inside of the bowl, add chocolate; gently fold in sifted flour until just combined. Transfer to a medium bowl.

3 Beat egg whites in a medium bowl with an electric mixer until soft peaks form. Fold egg whites into chocolate mixture, in two batches, until just combined. Spread mixture into pan.

4 Bake cake for 12 minutes or until golden and sponge springs back when pressed lightly with a finger.

5 Meanwhile, place a piece of baking paper, cut just larger than the pan, on a work surface; sprinkle evenly with extra sugar. Turn hot sponge onto sugar-covered-paper, peel away lining paper; trim crisped edges with a sharp knife. Working quickly, and using paper as a guide, roll sponge up from a long side. Cool for 5 minutes. Unroll sponge, remove paper; reroll, cover with a clean tea towel. Cool.

6 Meanwhile, combine strawberries, sifted icing sugar and half the sumac in a medium bowl. Cover; refrigerate for 30 minutes.

7 Beat mascarpone and cream in a small bowl with an electric mixer until almost firm peaks form.

8 Unroll cooled sponge; spread with two-thirds of the cream mixture, leaving a 2.5cm (1-inch) border on all sides. Top with half the meringue and half the strawberry mixture. Reroll sponge to enclose filling. Serve roulade topped with remaining cream, meringue and strawberry mixture; sprinkle with remaining sumac.

TIP To even out the shape or lessen any cracks in the roulade, simply roll it up in baking paper and tighten the ends like a bon bon; refrigerate for 20 minutes.

DO-AHEAD Roulade is best made on the day of serving.

Raspberry and rosewater pink velvet marshmallow cake
[RECIPE PAGES 142 & 143]

Layers of *Fragrant* girly colour smothered in *pillowy* sweetness

Raspberry and rosewater
PINK VELVET MARSHMALLOW CAKE

PREP + COOK TIME 1 HOUR 40 MINUTES (+ COOLING) SERVES 8

250g (8 ounces) butter, softened, chopped

6 egg whites

2 teaspoons vanilla extract

2 cups (440g) caster (superfine) sugar

2¹/₂ cups (375g) plain (all-purpose) flour

1 cup (250ml) buttermilk

2 teaspoons bicarbonate of soda (baking soda)

2 teaspoons white vinegar

3 teaspoons rose pink food colouring

185g (6 ounces) raspberries

RASPBERRY ROSEWATER CREAM

185g (6 ounces) raspberries

1 tablespoon rosewater

300ml thickened (heavy) cream

¹/₄ cup (40g) icing (confectioners') sugar

ROSEWATER MARSHMALLOW

³/₄ cup (165g) caster (superfine) sugar

1 tablespoon glucose syrup

2 tablespoons water

3 teaspoons rosewater

3 egg whites

1 Preheat oven to 180°C/350°F. Grease two 20cm (8-inch) round cake pans; line base and side with three layers of baking paper.

2 Beat butter in a large bowl with an electric mixer until smooth. Add egg whites, extract, sugar, flour and buttermilk.

3 Stir soda and vinegar in a small bowl until foamy; stir in colouring. Add to butter mixture. Beat on low speed until ingredients are combined. Beat on medium speed 2 minutes or until mixture turns a paler colour (mixture may look slightly curdled at this stage). Divide mixture between pans.

4 Bake cakes for 45 minutes or until a skewer inserted into the centre comes out clean. Stand cake in pans for 5 minutes before turning, top-side down, onto wire racks covered with greased baking paper to cool. Split cakes in half (see TECHNIQUES).

5 Make raspberry rosewater cream.

6 Place one cake layer on a plate, spread with one-third of the raspberry rosewater cream, leaving a 1cm (¹/₂-inch) border around edge. Repeat layering with remaining cakes and raspberry rosewater cream, finishing with cake.

7 Make rosewater marshmallow. Working quickly, use a metal spatula to spread marshmallow over top and side of cake, making peaks and swirls. Serve cake with raspberries.

RASPBERRY ROSEWATER CREAM Crush raspberries lightly with rosewater in a small bowl. Beat cream and sugar in a small bowl with an electric mixer until firm peaks form. Fold raspberry mixture through cream mixture.

ROSEWATER MARSHMALLOW Stir $^2/_3$ cup (150g) sugar, glucose, the water and rosewater in a small saucepan over medium heat without boiling until sugar dissolves. Bring to the boil; boil 3 minutes or until syrup reaches 115°C/239°F on a candy thermometer (or when a small amount of syrup dropped into a cup of cold water can be rolled into a soft ball). Remove pan from heat to allow the bubbles to subside. Meanwhile, beat egg whites in a small bowl of an electric mixer until soft peaks form; beat in remaining sugar until dissolved. With motor operating, add hot syrup in a thin stream, beating on high speed for 5 minutes or until mixture is thick and cooled. Use immediately.

TIPS You will need to work quickly when covering the cake with the rosewater marshmallow to preserve its texture. We used a water-based food colouring from supermarkets. Add drops of the colouring gradually to the batter using a skewer. When deciding on how intense you want the colour, bear in mind some intensity will be lost during baking. The colour also changes on the base and top of the cooked cake, giving it an almost marbled appearance when the cake is cut.

TECHNIQUES Step 1: see *'lining a round cake pan'*, page 276. Step 4: see also *'splitting a cake into even layers'*, page 277.

DO-AHEAD The cakes can be made a day ahead; store in an airtight container at room temperature. Fill and decorate on the day of serving; keep in a cool place, or refrigerate for up to 3 hours. Stand at room temperature for 1 hour before serving.

[PHOTOGRAPH PAGES 140 & 141]

Raspberry and rosewater
PINK VELVET MARSHMALLOW CAKE

[RECIPE PAGES 142 & 143]

MAKING THE CAKE

The cake batter is unusual with the additions of vinegar and bicarbonate of soda (baking soda). Together they react producing carbon dioxide, which gives the cake extra lightness. As you beat or stir the tinted vinegar mixture into the cake mixture, it might look a little curdled (this is okay) and quite brightly coloured – the intensity of the colour will lessen during cooking.

SPLITTING THE CAKE

Using a ruler, mark cuts halfway at several points around each cake. Holding the knife horizontally, cut through the cake using the scored marks as a guide. If you are nervous about splitting cakes or don't have a good serrated knife, freeze the cakes first for 30 minutes to firm the crumb, making it easier to cut through.

MAKING THE RASPBERRY ROSEWATER CREAM

Crush the raspberries with the rosewater using the back of a fork. If you don't have rosewater, add a little lemon juice. Fold raspberry mixture through the whipped cream mixture.

LAYERING THE CAKE

Place one cake layer on a cake plate
(see *'decorating cakes without a mess'*,
page 277). Spread cake with one-third
of the raspberry rosewater cream
using either the back of a spoon
or a palette knife. Repeat layering,
finishing with the final cake layer.

MAKING THE
ROSEWATER MARSHMALLOW

To check that the marshmallow mixture is
sufficiently beaten, feel the temperature of
the side of the bowl; it should feel barely
warm. Also, lift the beaters up, the mixture
should stick to the beaters in very thick,
stiff glossy peaks.

COVERING THE
CAKE AND SERVING

Spread the marshmallow quickly
over the top and side of the cake,
swirling it as you spread. Cut
the cake using a greased knife,
wiping the blade in between cuts
with paper towel.

Berry and lime cake
WITH WHIPPED COCONUT CREAM

PREP + COOK TIME 1 HOUR (+ REFRIGERATION & STANDING) SERVES 10

You will need to chill the coconut cream overnight before you start this recipe.

270ml (9 fluid ounces) canned coconut cream
20g (³/₄ ounce) butter, melted
2 limes
185g (6 ounces) butter, softened
1¹/₂ cups (330g) caster (superfine) sugar
4 eggs
1 cup (150g) plain (all-purpose) flour
¹/₂ cup (75g) self-raising flour
¹/₂ cup (40g) desiccated coconut
¹/₂ cup (125ml) buttermilk
1 cup (150g) mixed frozen berries
1 cup (250ml) thickened (heavy) cream
125g (4 ounces) raspberries
¹/₂ cup (25g) coconut flakes, toasted

1 Chill unopened can of coconut cream overnight.

2 Preheat oven to 160°C/325°F fan-forced. Brush a 24cm (9¹/₂-inch) bundt pan well with melted butter.

3 Finely grate rind from limes; reserve, separately, 2 teaspoons rind for cake and 1 teaspoon rind for whipped coconut cream. Juice 1 lime; you will need 2 tablespoons juice.

4 Beat butter and sugar in a small bowl with an electric mixer until pale and fluffy. Beat in eggs, one at a time, until just combined (mixture may look curdled at this stage). Transfer to a large bowl; stir in sifted flours, desiccated coconut, buttermilk, frozen berries, reserved rind and juice. Spoon mixture into pan; smooth surface.

5 Bake cake for 50 minutes or until a skewer inserted into the centre comes out clean. Stand cake in pan for 5 minutes before turning out onto a wire rack to cool.

6 Meanwhile, open chilled can of coconut cream; spoon ¹/₂ cup of the thick cream on the surface into a small bowl of an electric mixer (store remaining cream for another use). Add cream and remaining reserved rind; beat until soft peaks form.

7 Spoon half the whipped coconut cream on top of the cake; decorate with raspberries and flaked coconut. Serve cake with remaining whipped coconut cream.

TIP Instead of coconut flakes you could peel strips from the flesh of a freshly cracked coconut (as pictured).
DO-AHEAD This cake is best made on the day of serving.

BERRIES

Strawberries have two seasons, summer and winter in Australia, due to our different climatic areas. However, most berries are in season during summer and therefore at their cheapest. In many recipes frozen berries may be used, especially if they're in the cake batter. Care should be taken to substitute them in frostings as the extra water content might alter the consistency.

Washing BERRIES

WASH STRAWBERRIES ONLY WHEN YOU PLAN TO USE THEM WITH THEIR CALYXES (GREEN TOPS ON) TO REMOVE RESIDUAL PESTICIDES; THEN DRAIN ON PAPER TOWELS. BLUEBERRIES AND RASPBERRIES DON'T REQUIRE WASHING. FOR RASPBERRIES INSPECT THE HOLLOWS AS THE OCCASIONAL INSECT OR LEAF PART CAN SOMETIMES BE FOUND THERE.

IMPROVING THE FLAVOUR OF BERRIES *Lemon juice is much like salt in the cooking world in that it can be used to amplify and improve flavours. Add a splash to berries if they're a little lacklustre, along with some sugar.*

Storing BERRIES

Berries are highly perishable so should ideally be used within a day. Should you find one mouldy berry within a punnet ensure you discard it quickly to prevent mould spreading through the punnet. Surplus berries can be frozen on a tray then popped into bags or containers for use at another time.

DO AHEAD CREAM CAKES

Any cake that is to be topped with cream or that contains mostly cream in the filling is usually best assembled just before serving.

LOW FAT CREAM OPTIONS

If you would like a less rich accompaniment to a cake, try whipping half thickened cream and half Greek-style yoghurt together. Or even processing ricotta with a little icing (confectioners') sugar until it is smooth.

Whipping Cream

TO WHIP/BEAT CREAM IT NEEDS TO CONTAIN A CERTAIN PERCENTAGE OF BUTTER FAT, USUALLY AROUND 35%. FOR THIS REASON LIGHT (LOW-FAT) CREAMS (18%) CAN'T BE WHIPPED. CONVERSELY, CARE NEEDS TO BE TAKEN WITH CREAM CONTAINING A HIGH PERCENTAGE OF BUTTER FAT (48%-56%) AS THEY ARE EASILY OVERBEATEN AND ARE GENERALLY BETTER DEALT WITH BY HAND. CREAM DESIGNED FOR WHIPPING (THICKENED CREAM) CONTAINS EITHER GELATINE OR OTHER STABILISERS TO HELP HOLD THE WHIPPED CREAM TOGETHER BETTER.

KITCHEN BLOWTORCHES *A kitchen blowtorch trumps a grill (broiler) when it comes to browning meringue and caramelising fruit. They are readily available from kitchenware and hardware stores. When the canister gets low on gas, be careful not to tilt it too much or it will be hard to direct the flame. Instead you may need to elevate the item you are caramelising.*

PERFECT PEAKS

Pouring and thickened (heavy) cream needs to be chilled to whip well. On a hot day or when large amounts are to be whipped, chill the beaters and preferably a stainless steel bowl, in the freezer for 10 minutes. Always stop beating just before you think it's reached the desired stage to check, remembering that the cream will 'set' a little once you've finished.

MASCARPONE

Strictly speaking mascarpone is a cheese, however because of its soft consistency, it tends to be used as a cream. The texture can vary between brands; if yours is particularly thick, add a little pouring cream to it and take care not to overbeat it or it will curdle.

Raspberry crumble RING CAKE

PREP + COOK TIME 1 HOUR 30 MINUTES SERVES 10

125g (4 ounces) butter, softened

1¼ cups (275g) caster (superfine) sugar

1 teaspoon finely grated lemon rind

1 teaspoon vanilla bean paste

3 eggs

1 cup (150g) plain (all-purpose) flour

½ cup (75g) self-raising flour

¼ teaspoon bicarbonate of soda (baking soda)

½ cup (125ml) milk

125g (4 ounces) raspberries

1 teaspoon icing (confectioners') sugar

ALMOND CRUMBLE TOPPING

1 cup (150g) plain (all-purpose) flour

½ cup (60g) ground almonds

⅓ cup (75g) demerara sugar

⅓ cup (75g) caster (superfine) sugar

125g (4 ounces) cold butter, chopped

¼ cup (20g) rolled oats

⅓ cup (25g) flaked almonds

1 Preheat oven to 180°C/350°F. Grease a deep (10cm/4-inch) 20cm (8-inch) tube pan with removable base.

2 Beat butter, sugar, rind and paste in a small bowl with an electric mixer until pale and fluffy. Beat in eggs, one at a time, until just combined. Add combined sifted dry ingredients and milk; beat on low speed until just combined. Increase speed to medium; beat for 1 minute or until mixture is smooth and paler in colour. Spoon mixture into pan; smooth surface.

3 Bake cake for 20 minutes.

4 Meanwhile, make crumble topping.

5 Working quickly, scatter raspberries over cake, pushing them lightly into the mixture; sprinkle with topping.

6 Bake cake a further 30 minutes or until a skewer inserted into the centre comes out clean. Stand cake in pan for 10 minutes before transferring to a wire rack to cool. Dust with icing sugar.

ALMOND CRUMBLE TOPPING Combine flour, ground almonds and sugars in a large bowl. Rub in butter until mixture resembles fine breadcrumbs. Add oats and flaked almonds; press mixture together with your fingers to create large uneven lumps.

DO-AHEAD This cake is best made on day of serving.

Poppy seed
AND HAZELNUT CAKE
with raspberry mascarpone

PREP + COOK TIME 2 HOURS (+ STANDING) SERVES 16

$^1/_2$ cup (75g) poppy seeds

1 cup (250ml) milk

250g (8 ounces) unsalted butter, softened

2 cups (440g) caster (superfine) sugar

6 eggs

2 cups (300g) self-raising flour

2 cups (240g) ground hazelnuts

1 cup (240g) sour cream

500g (1 pound) mascarpone

300ml pouring cream

$^1/_2$ cup (80g) icing (confectioners') sugar

200g (6$^1/_2$ ounces) dark (semi-sweet) chocolate, chopped finely

375g (12 ounces) raspberries

1 Preheat oven to 160°C/320°F. Grease two 20cm (8-inch) round cake pans; line bases and sides with baking paper.

2 Place poppy seeds and milk in a small bowl; soak 15 minutes.

3 Beat butter and sugar in a medium bowl with an electric mixer for 6 minutes or until pale and fluffy. Beat in eggs, one at a time, until just combined. Add flour, ground hazelnuts, sour cream, and poppy seed mixture; beat on low speed until just combined. Spoon mixture evenly between pans.

4 Bake cakes for 1$^1/_4$ hours, swapping pans from top to bottom halfway during cooking time, or until a skewer inserted into the centre comes out clean. Stand cakes in pans for 5 minutes before turning, top-side up, onto baking-paper-covered wire racks to cool.

5 Beat mascarpone, $^1/_2$ cup of the cream and sifted icing sugar in a medium bowl with an electric mixer until firm peaks form.

6 Place chocolate and remaining cream in a small saucepan; stir over low heat until melted and smooth. Cool for 5 minutes.

7 Level cakes; split each cake into two layers (see TECHNIQUES). Reserve 60g (2 ounces) raspberries for top. Place one cake layer on a cake stand; spread with one-third of the mascarpone mixture, then top with one-third of the remaining raspberries, squeezing them lightly to flatten. Repeat layering with remaining cake layers, mascarpone mixture and raspberries, finishing with a cake layer. Spread top of cake with chocolate mixture, allowing some to drizzle down the side. Decorate with reserved raspberries.

TECHNIQUES Step 1: see *'lining a round cake pan'*, page 276. Step 7: see *'levelling a cake'*, page 277 and *'splitting a cake into even layers'*, page 277.

DO-AHEAD The cakes can be made 2 days ahead; store in an airtight container at room temperature.

Blackberry lemon cake
WITH BLACKBERRY FOOL

PREP + COOK TIME **1 HOUR 30 MINUTES (+ COOLING)** SERVES **8**

125g (4 ounces) butter, softened

$^3/_4$ cups (165g) caster (superfine) sugar

1 tablespoon finely grated lemon rind

2 eggs

1 cup (150g) self-raising flour

$^1/_2$ cup (60g) ground almonds

125g (4 ounces) sour cream

150g ($4^1/_2$ ounces) frozen blackberries

2 tablespoons lemon juice

2 tablespoons water

$^1/_3$ cup (75g) caster (superfine) sugar, extra

1 tablespoon icing (confectioners') sugar

1 cup (250ml) thickened (heavy) cream

1 Preheat oven 170°C/340°F. Grease a 11cm x 26cm ($4^1/_2$-inch x $10^1/_2$-inch) loaf pan; line base and long sides with baking paper, extending the paper 4cm ($1^1/_2$-inches) above the sides.

2 Beat butter, caster sugar and rind in a large bowl with an electric mixer until pale and fluffy. Beat in eggs, one at a time, until combined. Fold in sifted flour, then ground almonds and sour cream. Spoon half the mixture into pan; top with $^1/_4$ cup of the blackberries, pressing lightly into the mixture. Top with remaining cake mixture and another $^1/_4$ cup of the blackberries; smooth surface. Tap pan on a work surface to settle mixture.

3 Bake cake for 1 hour 10 minutes or until a skewer inserted in the centre comes out clean. Stand cake in pan for 10 minutes.

4 Meanwhile, stir juice, the water and extra caster sugar in a small saucepan over medium heat until sugar dissolves. Bring to the boil. Reduce heat; simmer for 2 minutes. Cool for 5 minutes.

5 Pour hot syrup over cake in pan. Stand for 20 minutes before transferring to a wire rack to cool completely.

6 Combine remaining berries and any juices with icing sugar in a small bowl; set aside to completely thaw. Crush lightly with a fork.

7 Beat cream in a large bowl with an electric mixer until soft peaks form.

8 Spoon cream on top of cake, drizzle with remaining berry mixture swirling lightly through cream.

TIP We used a loaf pan with a capacity of 1.5 litres (6 cups).
DO-AHEAD This cake is best made on day of serving.

Blueberry lemon
MERINGUE CHEESECAKE

PREP + COOK TIME 1 HOUR 50 MINUTES (+ REFRIGERATION & COOLING) SERVES 12

250g (8 ounces) butternut snap biscuits
60g (2 ounces) butter, melted
375g (12 ounces) cream cheese, softened
3/4 cup (165g) caster (superfine) sugar
2 teaspoons finely grated lemon rind
2 eggs, separated
1 tablespoon cornflour (cornstarch)
250g (8 ounces) mascarpone
2 tablespoons lemon juice
250g (8 ounces) store-bought lemon curd, chilled
250g (8 ounces) fresh blueberries
1 teaspoon icing (confectioners') sugar

MERINGUE
6 egg whites
1 3/4 cups (385g) caster (superfine) sugar

1 Preheat oven to 150°C/300°F.
2 Process biscuits until fine; add butter, process until combined. Spoon mixture evenly over base of a 22cm (9-inch) springform pan; press down firmly with a straight-sided glass or bottle. Place pan on an oven tray; refrigerate until required.
3 Beat cream cheese, 1/2 cup of the caster sugar, rind, egg yolks and cornflour in a large bowl with an electric mixer until smooth. Add mascarpone and juice; beat until just combined.
4 Beat egg whites in a small bowl with an electric mixer until soft peaks form. Gradually add remaining caster sugar, beating until dissolved. Fold egg white mixture into cream cheese mixture. Spoon mixture into crust.

5 Bake cheesecake for 50 minutes or until slightly soft in the centre. Cool in the oven with the door ajar.
6 Transfer cheesecake from pan to a cake plate. Spread lemon curd on cheesecake; top with two-thirds of the blueberries.
7 Make meringue.
8 Spoon one-third of the meringue into a piping bag fitted with a 1cm (1/2-inch) plain tube. Pipe meringue around cheesecake to cover the side. Squeeze any remaining meringue from piping bag back into the bowl of remaining meringue. Drop spoonfuls of remaining meringue on blueberries (see page 159 for how to make meringue quenelles). Using a blowtorch, lightly brown the meringue. Top cheesecake with remaining blueberries; dust with sifted icing sugar.

MERINGUE Beat egg whites and sugar in a large bowl with an electric mixer for 8 minutes or until thick and glossy.

TIPS Butternut snap biscuits don't need a lot of added butter to keep the crumbs together. If you use another type of biscuit, add extra melted butter gradually until the crumbs come together. Plain sweet biscuits may need up to 125g (4 ounces) butter. We have used store-bought lemon curd in this recipe but you can make your own using the recipe on page 50. Blowtorches are available from kitchenware and hardware stores. To serve, cut the cheesecake with a hot dry knife, wiping the blade clean between cuts with paper towel.
DO-AHEAD The cheesecake can be made a day ahead; keep refrigerated. Allow cheesecake to come to room temperature before serving.

Blueberry lemon
MERINGUE CHEESECAKE

[RECIPE PAGE 156]

MAKING THE CRUMB CRUST

Use a straight-side glass or bottle to press the crumb crust firmly and evenly over the base of the pan.

MAKING THE CHEESECAKE LAYER

Fold the mascarpone and juice into the cream cheese mixture, using a large metal spoon and a gentle folding action.

ADDING THE LEMON CURD LAYER AND BLUEBERRIES

Release the cheesecake from the side of the springform pan. You can leave the cake on the base if you prefer or transfer to a serving plate. Spread lemon curd evenly on top of cheesecake, then top with blueberries.

MAKING MERINGUE QUENELLES

Using a dessert spoon, scoop up a spoonful of the meringue mixture. Position a second dessert spoon, upside down, over the meringue; scoop under then over meringue, shaping it into a quenelle and transferring it to the second spoon. Using the first spoon, scoop under the quenelle-shaped meringue to push it onto the top of the cheesecake.

BROWNING THE MERINGUE

Before you start, ensure nothing flammable is near the cake, and that the plate or stand on which the cake is standing is flameproof. Hold the blowtorch about 20cm (8 inches) away from the meringue, aiming it first at the side; move the blowtorch in slow, sweeping movements around the side, then over the top, until meringue is lightly and evenly browned.

SERVING

Cut the cake using a hot, dry knife, wiping the blade in between cuts with paper towel.

Strawberry and Passionfruit FRANGIPANE CAKE

PREP + COOK TIME 50 MINUTES (+ REFRIGERATION & COOLING) SERVES 12

200g (6¹/₂ ounces) butter, softened

²/₃ cup (150g) caster (superfine) sugar

2 teaspoons finely grated orange rind

1 egg

¹/₂ cup (60g) ground almonds

¹/₂ cup (75g) self-raising flour

¹/₄ cup (35g) plain (all-purpose) flour

¹/₄ cup (45g) rice flour

¹/₂ cup (40g) flaked almonds

²/₃ cup (180ml) thickened (heavy) cream

¹/₄ cup (60g) crème fraîche

¹/₄ cup passionfruit pulp

LIQUEUR STRAWBERRIES

375g (12 ounces) strawberries, halved

2 tablespoons orange-flavoured liqueur

2 tablespoons caster (superfine) sugar

1 Make liqueur strawberries.

2 Preheat oven to 180°C/350°F. Grease a 12cm x 35cm (4³/₄-inch x 14-inch) rectangular loose-based tart tin.

3 Beat butter, sugar and rind in a medium bowl with an electric mixer until just combined. Beat in egg. Stir in ground almonds and sifted flours. Spread mixture into tin; sprinkle with flaked almonds, pressing down firmly.

4 Bake cake for 30 minutes or until a skewer inserted into the centre comes out clean. Cool in tin.

5 Beat cream and crème fraîche in a small bowl with an electric mixer until soft peaks form.

6 Drain liqueur strawberries over a small bowl; stir passionfruit into syrup.

7 Place cake on a long platter. Just before serving, top with cream mixture, then strawberries. Drizzle with passionfruit syrup.

LIQUEUR STRAWBERRIES Combine ingredients in a medium bowl; refrigerate for 1 hour, stirring occasionally.

TIP You will need about 3 passionfruit for this recipe.

DO-AHEAD The cake base can be made a day ahead; store in an airtight container at room temperature. Assemble cake just before serving.

INDULGENT CAKES

Ginger
& SPICE

Warming notes of *Ginger and spice* blend *Beautifully* to make all things *Nice*

Spiced tea cake
WITH HONEY FROSTING

PREP + COOK TIME 1 HOUR 45 MINUTES (+ COOLING & REFRIGERATION) SERVES 12

³/₄ cup (180ml) milk

1 vanilla bean, split lengthways (see TECHNIQUES)

4 chai tea bags

150g (4¹/₂ ounces) butter, softened

1 cup (220g) firmly packed brown sugar

3 eggs

2 cups (300g) self-raising flour

¹/₂ teaspoon ground cinnamon

¹/₄ teaspoon ground cardamom

60g (2 ounces) glacé ginger, sliced thinly

2 tablespoons honey

GINGER SYRUP

3cm (1¹/₄-inch) piece fresh ginger (15g), grated

2 tablespoons caster (superfine) sugar

¹/₃ cup (80ml) water

HONEY FROSTING

1¹/₂ cups (240g) icing (confectioners') sugar

500g (1 pound) cream cheese, softened

125g (4 ounces) butter, softened

¹/₃ cup (115g) honey

1 Preheat oven to 180°C/350°F. Grease a deep 20cm (8-inch) round cake pan; line base and side with three layers of baking paper.

2 Bring milk to the boil in a small saucepan. Remove from heat; scrape seeds from vanilla bean into pan, add bean and tea bags. Stand for 5 minutes. Discard bean and tea bags.

3 Beat butter and sugar in a small bowl with an electric mixer until paler and fluffy. Beat in eggs, one at a time, until just combined. Fold in sifted flour, ground spices and milk mixture. Spoon mixture into pan.

4 Bake cake for 50 minutes or until a skewer inserted in the centre comes out clean. Stand cake in pan for 15 minutes before turning, top-side up, onto a wire rack to cool.

5 Meanwhile, make ginger syrup, then honey frosting.

6 Split cake into three layers (see TECHNIQUES). Place the bottom cake layer on a cake plate; brush with one-third of the syrup, then spread with one-third of the frosting. Top with middle cake layer; brush with another third of the syrup and frosting. Finish with the top layer of cake, brushing the underside with remaining syrup; spread top with remaining frosting. Decorate with glacé ginger and drizzle with honey.

GINGER SYRUP Stir ingredients in a small saucepan over low heat, without boiling, until sugar dissolves. Bring to the boil; boil, without stirring, for 1 minute. Strain syrup into a small jug; discard ginger.

HONEY FROSTING Process ingredients until smooth and combined. Refrigerate for 20 minutes or until slightly firm.

TECHNIQUES Step 1: see *'lining a round cake pan'*, page 276.
Step 2: see *'preparing vanilla beans'*, page 276.
Step 6: see *'splitting a cake into even layers'*, page 277.
DO-AHEAD The cake is best made on day of serving but can be assembled 4 hours ahead; keep covered in the refrigerator.

chai parfait with
FIG AND WHOLE SPICE SYRUP

PREP + COOK TIME 1 HOUR (+ COOLING, REFRIGERATION & FREEZING) SERVES 6

You will need an empty 1 litre cardboard milk carton to mould the parfait in. Alternatively you can use a 1 litre (4-cup) terrine tin.

1$^1/_2$ cups (375ml) milk
2$^1/_2$ tablespoons good-quality loose-leaf black tea
2 star anise
10 cloves
1 cinnamon stick, broken in half
2 cardamon pods, bruised
2cm ($^3/_4$-inch) piece fresh ginger (10g), grated finely
300ml pouring cream
8 egg yolks
$^1/_2$ cup (110g) caster (superfine) sugar
2 ginger nut biscuits (30g), crushed coarsely
2 tablespoons pistachios, chopped coarsely
$^1/_4$ cup (35g) glacé ginger, chopped coarsely

FIG AND WHOLE SPICE SYRUP
$^1/_2$ cup (110g) firmly packed brown sugar
$^1/_2$ cup (125ml) water
3 cardamom pods
4 black peppercorns
6 cloves
6 allspice
1 star anise
1 cinnamon stick, broken in half
100g (3 ounces) dried wild figs
2 teaspoons freshly squeezed orange juice

1 Heat milk in a large heavy-based saucepan until almost boiling. Remove from heat; stir in tea, spices and ginger until combined. Stand for 15 minutes. Pour through a sieve; discard solids.

2 Return strained milk to pan, stir in cream; bring almost to the boil. Meanwhile, whisk egg yolks and sugar in a medium bowl until pale. Gradually whisk hot milk mixture into egg yolk mixture until combined. Return mixture to pan; stir continuously over low heat until custard thickens enough to coat the back of a spoon (do not allow to boil).

3 Pour custard into a medium stainless steel bowl, place bowl over a second larger bowl filled with ice; whisk custard for a few minutes to cool slightly. Cover surface with plastic wrap; refrigerate until chilled.

4 Churn chilled custard in an ice-cream machine, following manufacturer's directions. Five minutes before end of churning, add biscuits, nuts and glacé ginger; churn a further 5 minutes or until incorporated.

5 Pour ice-cream into a clean 1 litre (4 cup) cardboard milk carton; seal top. Freeze, standing carton upright, for 6 hours or overnight.

6 Make fig and whole spice syrup.

7 To serve, remove parfait from freezer and tear away cardboard milk carton. Place on a platter with a lip; spoon over fig and whole spice syrup.

FIG AND WHOLE SPICE SYRUP Place ingredients, except juice, in a small heavy-based saucepan over low heat; stir for 1 minute until sugar dissolves. Bring to the boil. Reduce heat; simmer for 12 minutes or until figs have softened and syrup thickened slightly. Cool, then stir in juice. Cut half the figs in half.

TIPS To crush ginger nuts, place in a metal or plastic bowl and use the end of a rolling pin to crush them; sift to remove any fine crumbs. Avoid eating whole spices as these are left in the syrup as a garnish only, the figs however will be delicious.

DO-AHEAD Parfait can be made a day ahead.

[PHOTOGRAPH PAGES 168 & 169]

Spiced sponge
AND RHUBARB ROULADE

PREP + COOK TIME 45 MINUTES (+ COOLING) SERVES 10

5 eggs, separated
$^2/_3$ cup (150g) caster (superfine) sugar
$1^1/_2$ tablespoons hot water
80g ($2^1/_2$ ounces) white chocolate, grated finely
$^2/_3$ cup (100g) self-raising flour
1 teaspoon ground cinnamon
$^1/_2$ teaspoon ground nutmeg
$^1/_4$ teaspoon ground cloves
$^1/_4$ teaspoon ground cardamom
$^1/_4$ cup (55g) caster (superfine) sugar, extra

ROASTED RHUBARB
500g (1 pound) rhubarb, trimmed,
    cut into 5cm (2-inch) lengths
$^1/_3$ cup (75g) firmly packed brown sugar
2 teaspoons finely grated orange rind
1 tablespoon orange juice
2.5cm (1-inch) piece fresh ginger (12.5g), grated

MASCARPONE CREAM
$^1/_2$ cup (125ml) thickened (heavy) cream
1 cup (250g) mascarpone

1 Preheat oven to 200°C/400°F. Grease a 26cm x 32cm
($10^1/_2$-inch x $12^3/_4$-inch) swiss roll pan; line base with baking
paper, extending the paper 5cm (2 inches) over the long sides.
2 Beat egg yolks and sugar in a medium bowl with an electric
mixer for 5 minutes or until very thick. Pour the hot water down
inside of the bowl, add chocolate; gently fold in combined sifted
flour and spices until just combined. Transfer to a medium bowl.

3 Beat egg whites in a medium bowl with an electric mixer
until soft peaks form. Fold egg whites into chocolate mixture,
in two batches, until just combined. Spread mixture into pan.
4 Bake cake for 12 minutes or until golden and sponge springs
back when pressed lightly with a finger.
5 Meanwhile, place a piece of baking paper, cut just larger than
the pan, on a work surface; sprinkle evenly with extra sugar.
Turn hot sponge onto sugar-covered-paper, peel away lining
paper; trim crisped edges with a sharp knife. Working quickly,
and using paper as a guide, roll sponge up from a long side.
Cool for 5 minutes. Unroll sponge, remove paper; reroll, cover
with a clean tea towel. Cool.
6 Meanwhile, make roasted rhubarb. Make mascarpone cream.
7 Unroll sponge; spread with mascarpone cream, leaving a
2.5cm (1-inch) border. Top with rhubarb. Reroll sponge to
enclose filling. Serve roulade drizzled with rhubarb pan juices.

ROASTED RHUBARB Combine ingredients in a medium bowl;
transfer to a small shallow baking dish. Roast in oven for
10 minutes, stirring halfway, or until rhubarb is tender.

MASCARPONE CREAM Beat cream and mascarpone in a small
bowl with an electric mixer until soft peaks form.

DO-AHEAD This recipe is best made on day of serving.

Spiced sponge
AND RHUBARB ROULADE

[RECIPE PAGE 172]

SIFTING THE FLOUR AND SPICES TOGETHER

Sift flour and spices together so they are well combined before folding them into the cake batter.

ROLLING THE ROULADE

While the sponge is warm and using the baking paper as a guide, roll up the spiced sponge from a long side. Leave for 5 minutes, then unroll. Doing this means that it will roll more easily, without cracking, once the sponge is cooled and filled.

MAKING THE ROASTED RHUBARB

Cut the trimmed rhubarb into 5cm (2-inch) lengths. If any pieces are particularly wide, cut them in half lengthways. Place rhubarb pieces in a roasting dish just large enough to fit all the ingredients in a single layer. Roast; stirring halfway through cooking.

MAKING THE MASCARPONE CREAM

Whisk the cream and mascarpone together until soft peaks form, taking care not to overbeat it.

ASSEMBLING THE ROULADE

The roulade will not be quite flat once unrolled, so when you spread on the mascarpone cream you will also need to spread it under the fold. Place rhubarb pieces on cream layer, also tucking pieces under the fold. Reroll the sponge using the paper as a guide.

SERVING

If there are any patches of moisture on the outside of the roulade, cover them with a little more caster sugar. Serve roulade immediately, cut into slices.

Triple ginger loaf

PREP + COOK TIME 1 HOUR 45 MINUTES (+ COOLING) SERVES 10

180g (5¹/₂ ounces) butter, chopped
¹/₃ cup (75g) firmly packed dark brown sugar
¹/₂ cup (175g) treacle
¹/₂ cup (175g) golden syrup
1 cup (250ml) milk
1¹/₂ teaspoons bicarbonate of soda (baking soda)
1²/₃ cups (300g) plain (all-purpose) flour
3 teaspoons ground ginger
1¹/₂ teaspoons ground allspice
³/₄ cup (165g) crystallised ginger, chopped
2 eggs, beaten lightly
¹/₄ teaspoon ground ginger, extra

GINGER ALE ICING
¹/₂ cup (125ml) ginger ale
20g (³/₄ ounce) butter
1 cups (160g) icing (confectioners') sugar
3 teaspoons lemon juice

1 Preheat oven to 160°C/325°F. Grease a 15cm x 23.5cm x 9cm (6-inch x 9¹/₂-inch x 3³/₄-inch) loaf pan; line base and sides with baking paper, extending the paper 5cm (2 inches) over the sides.
2 Stir butter, sugar, treacle, golden syrup and milk in a large saucepan over medium heat until butter melts and sugar dissolves. Bring to the boil (mixture may look slightly curdled at this stage). Remove from heat; stir in soda.
3 Sift flour and ground spices into a large bowl; stir in butter mixture and crystallised ginger until just combined. Stir in egg until just combined. Pour mixture into pan. Cover with a piece of pleated foil (see TIPS).
4 Bake loaf for 1 hour. Remove foil; bake a further 30 minutes or until a skewer inserted into the centre comes out with a few moist crumbs attached (the cake will have a crack along the top, however this is fine). Cool loaf in pan.
5 Make ginger ale icing; pour immediately over cooled cake. Stand cake until icing sets.
6 Serve loaf dusted with extra ground ginger.

GINGER ALE ICING Bring ginger ale to the boil in a small saucepan over medium heat; boil for 6 minutes or until reduced to 2 tablespoons. Remove from heat; stir in butter until melted. Transfer mixture to a small bowl; whisk in sifted icing sugar and 2 teaspoons of the juice until combined. Gradually stir in enough of the remaining juice, if needed, to thin the icing.

TIPS We used a loaf pan with a capacity of 3 litres (12 cups). Pleating the foil allows for the cake to expand as it cooks. To make the pleated foil, use a piece of foil slightly larger than the loaf pan. Fold the foil to create a pleat down the centre.
DO-AHEAD The uniced cake can be made a day ahead; store in an airtight container at room temperature.

Upside-down PINEAPPLE AND GINGER sour cream cake

PREP + COOK TIME **1 HOUR 45 MINUTES (+ COOLING)** SERVES **16**

250g (8 ounces) butter, softened

1³/₄ cups (385g) firmly packed brown sugar

5 eggs

1 cup (240g) sour cream

2 cups (300g) plain (all-purpose) flour

¹/₂ cup (75g) self-raising flour

1 tablespoon ground ginger

1 teaspoon ground cinnamon

¹/₂ teaspoon ground clove

4cm (1¹/₂-inch) piece fresh ginger (20g), sliced thinly

CARAMELISED PINEAPPLE

1 medium ripe pineapple (1.25kg)

85g (3 ounces) butter

³/₄ cup (165g) firmly packed brown sugar

1 Make caramelised pineapple.

2 Preheat oven to 170°C/340°F. Grease a deep 22cm (9-inch) square cake pan; line base and sides with baking paper, extending the paper 5cm (2-inches) over the sides.

3 Arrange caramelised pineapple slices, overlapping, on base of cake pan to cover; drizzle with 2 tablespoons of reserved syrup.

4 Beat butter and sugar in a medium bowl with an electric mixer until pale and fluffy. Beat in eggs, one at a time. Stir in sour cream and sifted dry ingredients. Carefully spread mixture over pineapple in pan; tap pan on bench to remove any large air bubbles.

5 Bake cake for 1 hour 25 minutes or until a skewer inserted into the centre comes out clean.

6 Meanwhile, add ginger to remaining reserved syrup in pan; bring to the boil. Reduce heat; simmer for 5 minutes or until thick and syrupy.

7 Stand cake in pan for 5 minutes before turning onto a cake plate or stand. Brush pineapple with a little of the warm syrup. Serve warm cake with remaining syrup.

CARAMELISED PINEAPPLE Trim top and bottom from pineapple; cut off the skin. Cut pineapple into quarters lenthways; remove the cores. Cut each quarter crossways into twelve 5mm (¹/₄-inch) thick slices; you will have 48 slices. (See TECHNIQUES.) Stir butter and sugar in a large frying pan over low heat until sugar dissolves. Bring to a simmer, add half the pineapple; simmer, turning pineapple, for 3 minutes, or just tender. Using a slotted spoon, transfer pineapple to a tray; cool. Repeat with remaining pineapple. Reserve syrup in pan.

TECHNIQUES Step 1: see also *'cutting pineapple'*, page 276.

Step 2: see *'lining a square cake pan'*, page 276.

DO-AHEAD This cake is best made on day of serving.

Pumpkin gingerbread cake

PREP + COOK TIME 2 HOURS 15 MINUTES (+ STANDING) SERVES 12

185g (6 ounces) butter, softened
2 teaspoons vanilla extract
5cm (2-inch) piece fresh ginger (25g), grated finely
1¼ cups (275g) firmly packed brown sugar
3 eggs
3 cups (450g) self-raising flour
3 teaspoons ground ginger
1 teaspoon ground cinnamon
½ teaspoon ground nutmeg
¼ teaspoon ground cloves
¼ teaspoon cooking salt
¾ teaspoon bicarbonate of soda (baking soda)
1 cup (250ml) buttermilk
1½ cups (350g) mashed butternut pumpkin
2 tablespoons thinly sliced crystallised ginger
2 tablespoons coarsely chopped roasted pecans

CARAMEL SAUCE
60g (2 ounces) butter
½ cup (110g) firmly packed brown sugar
2 tablespoons water
2 tablespoons dark rum

1 Preheat oven to 180°C/350°F. Grease a deep 22cm (9-inch) bundt pan.
2 Beat butter, extract, grated ginger and sugar in a large bowl with an electric mixer until paler and fluffy. Beat in eggs, one at a time, until just combined. Fold in combined sifted flour, ground spices, salt and soda with buttermilk, in two batches, until combined. Stir in pumpkin. Spread mixture into pan; batter should nearly fill the pan.
3 Bake cake on lowest oven shelf for 50 minutes or until a skewer inserted into the centre comes out clean. Stand cake in pan for 15 minutes before turning out onto a wire rack to cool. Level the base of the cake, if necessary (see TECHNIQUES).
4 Make caramel sauce.
5 Place cake on a cake stand or plate; drizzle with sauce. Decorate with crystallised ginger and pecans. Serve warm or cold.

CARAMEL SAUCE Stir butter, sugar and the water in a small saucepan over low heat, without boiling, until butter melts and sugar dissolves. Bring to the boil; boil for 3 minutes or until sauce thickens. Remove from heat; stir in rum. Stand sauce for 5 minutes to thicken.

TIPS You need to cook 1kg (2 pounds) pumpkin for the amount of mashed pumpkin needed. You can decorate this cake with Chinese candied ginger strips, available from Asian grocers.
TECHNIQUES Step 3: see *'levelling a cake'*, page 277.
DO-AHEAD The cake and syrup can be made a day ahead; store separately at room temperature.

Saffron honey syrup cakes
[RECIPE PAGES 184 & 185]

Saffron honey
SYRUP CAKES

PREP + COOK TIME **1 HOUR 15 MINUTES (+ REFRIGERATION & STANDING)** MAKES **12**

You will need to start this recipe a day ahead.

$^1/_4$ teaspoon loosely packed saffron threads

2 teaspoons lemon juice

1 vanilla bean

200g (6$^1/_2$ ounces) cultured unsalted butter, softened, chopped

2 teaspoons finely grated lemon rind

$^3/_4$ cup (165g) caster (superfine) sugar

3 eggs, separated

1$^2/_3$ cups (250g) self-raising flour

1 cup (280g) Greek-style yoghurt

$^1/_3$ cup (55g) roasted almonds, chopped

SWEET VANILLA LABNE

1 vanilla bean

1kg (2 pounds) Greek-style yoghurt

$^1/_2$ teaspoon salt

$^1/_3$ cup (115g) honey

HONEY SAFFRON SYRUP

$^1/_4$ teaspoon loosely packed saffron threads

$^3/_4$ cup (180ml) water

$^1/_4$ cup (90g) honey

$^3/_4$ cup (165g) caster (superfine) sugar

2 strips lemon rind

$^1/_3$ cup (80ml) lemon juice

6 cloves

2 cinnamon sticks

1 Make sweet vanilla labne.

2 Combine saffron and juice in a small bowl; stand for 20 minutes.

3 Meanwhile, preheat oven to 180°C/350°F. Grease 12 oval friand pans; line bases with baking paper.

4 Split vanilla bean in half lengthways; scrape seeds into a small bowl of an electric mixer (see TECHNIQUES). Reserve bean for honey saffron syrup. Add chopped butter to bowl with rind and sugar; beat 3 minutes or until pale and fluffy. Beat in egg yolks, one at a time, until combined. Transfer mixture to a large bowl. Stir in flour and yoghurt, in two batches; stir in saffron mixture.

5 Beat egg whites in a small bowl with an electric mixer until soft peaks form. Stir into cake mixture, in two batches. Spoon $1/3$ cup mixture into pan holes.

6 Bake cakes for 25 minutes or until a skewer inserted into the centre comes out clean.

7 Meanwhile, make honey saffron syrup.

8 Turn hot cakes, top-side up, onto a wire rack over an oven tray. Brush hot syrup over hot cakes. Serve cakes topped with labne and nuts, and drizzle with remaining syrup.

[PHOTOGRAPH PAGES 182 & 183]

SWEET VANILLA LABNE Split vanilla bean in half lengthways; scrape seeds into a medium bowl (see TECHNIQUES). Cut bean in half crossways, add to bowl with remaining ingredients; stir until combined. Spoon yoghurt mixture into a sieve lined with two layers of muslin or a clean Chux cloth. Tie cloth close to yoghurt. Refrigerate for 12 hours or overnight, squeezing the yoghurt occasionally, until thick. Remove vanilla bean pieces; stir yoghurt mixture until smooth.

HONEY SAFFRON SYRUP Stir ingredients and reserved vanilla bean in a small saucepan over medium heat until sugar dissolves. Bring to the boil. Remove from heat; stand 5 minutes. Discard whole spices.

TIP Cultured butter is available alongside regular butter.

TECHNIQUES Steps 1 & 4: see also *'preparing vanilla beans'*, page 276.

DO-AHEAD The cakes can be made a day ahead. Store in an airtight container at room temperature.

Saffron honey SYRUP CAKES

[RECIPE PAGES 184 & 185]

MAKING SWEET LABNE

Spoon yoghurt mixture into a sieve lined with a piece of muslin (or two new, well-rinsed Chux cloths). Gather all edges of the muslin, forming mixture into a tight ball, then tie tightly to secure and form a tight ball. Place back in the sieve over a bowl; excess whey will drain out, producing a thick yoghurt mixture (labne).

INFUSING THE SAFFRON FOR THE CAKES

Stir the saffron and lemon juice together in a small bowl and leave to stand for 20 minutes. This will soften the saffron threads and draw out the saffron flavour.

PREPARING THE FRIAND PAN

Grease friand pan holes. For an easy way to cut out the lining papers, fold a large piece of baking paper in half three times alternating the direction you fold, until there are eight layers. Staple around the edge of the stack to secure, place the stack under the pan, trace around the base a pan hole; cut around the outline, this will give you 8 ovals. Repeat with a second piece of paper only folding it twice to create four more ovals.

FILLING THE FRIAND PAN

Fill the friand pan holes equally. Use a measuring cup to scoop up $\frac{1}{3}$ cup of the batter, then using a spoon, scoop batter into lined holes.

CREAMING BUTTER AND SUGAR

Beat butter, sugar and vanilla, either by hand with a wooden spoon or with an electric mixer until light and fluffy. Beat in egg yolks, then stir in flour and yoghurt, in two batches, until just combined. Stir in the saffron and soaking liquid.

SERVING

Untie the labne and place spoonfuls on each cake, top with nuts and drizzle with remaining syrup.

SCALES

Precision is critical for baking, a little more of something, or a little less can throw a whole recipe out, so use scales to be super accurate. Not all though are created equal, if you're in the market for a new pair, buy a set that calibrates in 1 gram increments. Scales also speed up the weighing process if you use the tare button which zeros the scales.

Vanilla Beans

THREE THINGS TO DO WITH A SPENT VANILLA BEAN

(1) Make vanilla sugar: pop the rinsed and dried bean in a canister of caster (superfine) sugar and leave to infuse for at least a week.

(2) Make a sugar syrup, using twice as much water to sugar and a strip of orange rind, 5 cloves and a little lemon juice; stir until sugar dissolves; simmer for 5 minutes. Use for a fruit salad or to moisten a cake.

(3) Make vanilla hot chocolate: add the bean to milk, with real dark chocolate and slowly bring almost to the boil. Sweeten with a little honey or sugar.

WHY ARE VANILLA BEANS SO EXPENSIVE? *For starters, production is labour intensive and pollination must occur on the single day the flowers open. In Mexico, it's done by bees, elsewhere it must be done by hand, before the lengthy curing process is undertaken.*

WHAT IS THE BEST FORM OF VANILLA?

THERE ARE FOUR BASIC FORMS: ESSENCE, EXTRACT, PASTE AND THE WHOLE BEAN. ESSENCE IS OFTEN CHEMICALLY DERIVED FROM WOOD PULP AND HAS A HARSH TASTE. EXTRACT AND PASTE ARE SIMILAR IN FLAVOUR, CONVENIENT AND INEXPENSIVE. THE PASTE INCLUDES VISIBLE SEEDS MAKING IT A GOOD ALTERNATIVE IN RECIPES CALLING FOR THE BEAN. BEANS OFFER THE BEST FLAVOUR; THE MOST PRIZED ARE FROM MADAGASCAR.

FRESH IS BEST

To appreciate the best flavour spices have to offer, especially ground spices, buy them in small amounts and replace them regularly.

GINGER

New season ginger appears on greengrocer shelves in May. It's easy to spot with paper thin, pale skin. Ginger is at its most succulent and aromatic when fresh – it loses moisture and becomes more fibrous as it ages.

BRUISING
SPICES AND HERBS

BRUISING (WHICH IS ANOTHER WORD FOR LIGHTLY CRUSHING) SPICES OR HERBS SUCH AS CARDAMOM PODS AND LEMON GRASS. IT HELPS TO RELEASE THE FLAVOURS, WHICH ARE SOMETIMES CONTAINED IN THE SEEDS. HOLD A KNIFE HORIZONTALLY OVER THE SPICE, AND WITH THE HEEL OF YOUR HAND GIVE THE FLAT BLADE A WHACK TO CRUSH THE SPICE OR HERB. YOU CAN ALSO DO THIS WITH A MORTAR AND PESTLE.

STORE SPICES AWAY FROM HEAT OR LIGHT IN AIRTIGHT PACKETS OR CONTAINERS (NOT IN THE FRIDGE). ALL SPICES DETERIORATE OVER TIME, SO SHOULD BE CHECKED AT LEAST ONCE A YEAR.

REMOVING
SPICES
TO SERVE

It's up to you if you decide to do this. In many cultures, spices are left in as visual clues to the dish's flavour. If you do leave them in, just tell your guests that they are there, at the worst, if they forget and eat them, they'll get an intense hit of the spice.

a world of spices

Take care when using ground nutmeg, clove, cardamom and star anise as they are a lot more potent than other spices. However, in their whole form they offer more subtlety and can be used to infuse custards and syrups. In the spice world, cinnamon is the equivalent of vanilla, having an affinity with many things making it an ideal substitute if you don't have a particular spice.

Greek walnut and spice cake
WITH RED WINE PEARS

PREP + COOK TIME **1 HOUR 10 MINUTES** SERVES **8**

4 small firm corella pears (720g)

3 cups (660g) caster (superfine) sugar

3 cups (750ml) red wine

3 star anise

2 cinnamon sticks

300g (9¹/₂ ounces) walnuts, roasted lightly

1 cup (70g) fresh white breadcrumbs

1¹/₂ teaspoons baking powder

1 teaspoon ground cinnamon

¹/₄ teaspoon ground cloves

¹/₄ teaspoon ground star anise

4 eggs, separated

²/₃ cup (150g) caster (superfine) sugar

125g (4 ounces) butter, melted

1 Peel pears, keeping stalks attached; cut in half. Place sugar, wine, whole star anise and cinnamon sticks in a medium saucepan. Bring to the boil, over medium heat, stirring to dissolve sugar. Reduce heat to low; simmer for 5 minutes. Add pears; cover with a round of baking paper and a small heatproof plate to keep pears submerged. Simmer for 15 minutes or until just tender. Cool.

2 Preheat oven to 180°C/350°F. Grease a 22cm (9-inch) springform pan; line base and side with baking paper.

3 Pulse nuts in a food processor until finely chopped. Place nuts in a large bowl with breadcrumbs, baking powder and ground spices; stir until combined.

4 Beat egg yolks and sugar in a large bowl with an electric mixer until creamy. Add nut mixture; mix well. Fold in butter. Beat egg whites in a large bowl with an electric mixer until soft peaks form. Fold egg whites into cake mixture, in two batches. Pour mixture into pan.

5 Bake cake for 35 minutes or until a skewer inserted in the centre comes out clean. Stand cake in pan for 10 minutes before turning, top-side up, onto a wire rack to cool.

6 Place 2 cups of pear poaching liquid in a small saucepan; simmer, over medium heat, for 10 minutes or until thickened.

7 Place cake on a cake stand or plate; top with pears and syrup.

TECHNIQUES Step 2: see *'lining a round cake pan'*, page 276.
DO-AHEAD The cake and pears can be made a day ahead. Store cake in an airtight container at room temperature; pears and syrup in the refrigerator. Assemble on day of serving.

Pumpkin spice cake
WITH MAPLE FROSTING

PREP + COOK TIME **1 HOUR 40 MINUTES (+ COOLING)** SERVES **12**

2 eggs

$^3/_4$ cup (165g) firmly packed brown sugar

$^1/_4$ cup (60ml) maple syrup

$^2/_3$ cup (160ml) vegetable oil

2 cups (340g) firmly packed coarsely grated
butternut pumpkin

$^1/_2$ cup (60g) chopped pecans

$1^2/_3$ cups (250g) self-raising flour

$^1/_2$ teaspoon bicarbonate of soda (baking soda)

1 teaspoon ground allspice

2 teaspoons ground cinnamon

1 teaspoon ground ginger

$^1/_4$ teaspoon ground cinnamon, extra

SUGARED PECANS

1 cup (160g) pecan halves

$^1/_4$ cup (40g) icing (confectioners') sugar

MAPLE FROSTING

375g (12 ounces) cream cheese, softened, chopped

200g ($6^1/_2$ ounces) butter, softened

$^1/_3$ cup (80ml) maple syrup

2 cups (320g) icing (confectioners') sugar

1 Preheat oven to 180°C/350°F. Grease a 20cm x 30cm (8-inch x 12-inch) slice pan; line base and long sides with baking paper, extending the paper 5cm (2 inches) over edges.

2 Beat eggs, sugar, syrup and oil in a small bowl with an electric mixer for 5 minutes or until thick and creamy. Transfer mixture to a large bowl; stir in pumpkin and nuts, then sifted dry ingredients. Spread mixture into pan.

3 Bake cake for 30 minutes or until a skewer inserted into the centre comes out clean. Stand cake in pan for 5 minutes before turning, top-side up, onto a wire rack to cool.

4 Meanwhile, make sugared pecans, then maple frosting.

5 Split cake in half (see TECHNIQUES). Place the bottom cake layer on a cake plate; spread with half the frosting. Finish with top cake layer and remaining frosting. Decorate with sugared pecans; dust with extra ground cinnamon.

SUGARED PECANS Rinse nuts in a sieve under cold water until wet. Spread nuts, in a single layer, on a baking-paper-lined oven tray. Dust with sifted icing sugar. Roast in oven for 10 minutes or until browned lightly.

MAPLE FROSTING Beat cream cheese and butter in a small bowl with an electric mixer for 3 minutes or until fluffy and smooth. Gradually beat in syrup and sifted icing sugar until smooth and combined.

TIP You will need about half a small butternut pumpkin for the amount of grated pumpkin required.

TECHNIQUES Step 5: see also *'splitting a cake into even layers'*, page 277.

DO-AHEAD This cake can be made and frosted a day ahead; refrigerate. Stand at room temperature for at least 1 hour before serving. Sugared pecans can be made several days ahead; store in an airtight container at room temperature. Decorate cake with pecans just before serving.

Cardamom savarin with apricots in dessert wine syrup
[RECIPE PAGES 196 & 197]

Cardamom savarin with
APRICOTS IN DESSERT WINE SYRUP

PREP + COOK TIME 55 MINUTES (+ STANDING) SERVES 12

Most people have heard of a rum baba, a savarin is a version of the same yeasted, syrup-soaked dessert, cooked in a special ring-shaped pan of the same name. Here we have used a more readily available bundt pan for this spiced version.

2 teaspoons (7g) dried yeast

¼ cup (60ml) milk, lukewarm

2 tablespoons caster (superfine) sugar

4 eggs, beaten lightly

1¾ cups (260g) '00' flour, bread or plain (all-purpose) flour

1½ teaspoons sea salt flakes

1 teaspoon ground cardamom

100g (3 ounces) butter, softened, chopped

20g (¾ ounce) butter, extra, melted

APRICOTS IN DESSERT WINE SYRUP

1 medium orange (240g)

3 cups (750ml) dessert wine

2 cups (500ml) water

2½ cups (550g) caster (superfine) sugar

10 cardamom pods, bruised

1¼ cups (185g) dried apricot halves

1 Combine yeast, milk and 1 teaspoon of the sugar in a small bowl; cover, stand in a warm place 10 minutes or until frothy. Stir in egg.

2 Combine flour, salt, cardamom and remaining sugar in a large bowl of an electric mixer fitted with a dough hook. Add yeast mixture; mix on medium speed for 3 minutes or until dough is smooth and elastic. Scrape down the side of bowl with a spatula; cover, stand in a warm place for 1 hour or until dough has doubled in size.

3 Meanwhile, make apricots in dessert wine syrup.

4 Return the bowl with the risen dough to the electric mixer fitted with the dough hook. Add chopped butter to dough, a few pieces at a time, beating on medium speed, for 2 minutes or until smooth and elastic.

[PHOTOGRAPH PAGES 194 & 195]

5 Grease a 24cm (9½-inch) non-stick bundt pan well with the melted butter. Spoon dough mixture into a disposable piping bag; pipe mixture into pan. Cover loosely; stand in a warm place for 45 minutes or until mixture is almost doubled in size.
6 Preheat oven to 220°C/425°F.
7 Bake savarin for 25 minutes or until golden and a skewer inserted into the centre comes out clean. Stand savarin in pan for 5 minutes.
8 Strain apricots in syrup, reserving apricots, rind and cardamom. Pour 3 cups (750ml) of the syrup slowly over the savarin in the pan until syrup is absorbed. Stand savarin for 10 minutes before turning out onto a cake plate.
9 Meanwhile, simmer remaining syrup in a small saucepan over medium heat for 8 minutes or until thickened. Return reserved apricots, rind and cardamom to thickened syrup. Cool.
10 Serve savarin warm or at room temperature, with apricots and drizzled with thickened syrup.

APRICOTS IN DESSERT WINE SYRUP Using a vegetable peeler, peel rind from orange avoiding white pith; cut into thin strips (or use a zester). Place rind, wine, the water, sugar and cardamom in a medium saucepan; bring to the boil, stirring to dissolve sugar. Simmer 2 minutes. Cut half the apricots in half, add all apricots to syrup. Remove from heat; cover until needed.

TIP We used Brown's Orange Muscat Flora, a unique Australian dessert wine.
TO MAKE THE DOUGH BY HAND In step 2, stir ingredients together in a large bowl using a wooden spoon to form a sticky dough. Turn out onto a well-floured work surface and knead for 3 minutes or until smooth. Place in an oiled bowl and continue step 2. In step 4, turn the risen dough out onto a well-floured work surface, knead butter, piece-by-piece, into the dough, kneading well after each adition until all butter is incorporated and dough is smooth. Continue onto step 5.
DO-AHEAD This cake is best made on day of serving but keeps well for 2 days if refrigerated.

Ginger beer date cake
WITH CREAM CHEESE FROSTING

PREP + COOK TIME 2 HOURS 30 MINUTES (+ STANDING & COOLING) SERVES 12

1 cup (250ml) ginger beer
300g (9½ ounces) fresh dates, pitted, chopped
1 teaspoon bicarbonate of soda (baking soda)
250g (8 ounces) unsalted butter, softened
1¾ cups (385g) firmly packed brown sugar
4 eggs
3 cups (450g) plain (all-purpose) flour
1 teaspoon baking powder
¼ cup (60ml) milk
1 teaspoon vanilla extract

CREAM CHEESE FROSTING
500g (1 pound) cream cheese, softened, chopped
1 cup (220g) firmly packed brown sugar
3 teaspoons mixed spiced

1 Preheat oven to 170°C/340°F. Grease a 22cm (9-inch) square cake pan; line base and sides with three layers of baking paper.
2 Bring ginger beer to the boil in a small saucepan. Remove from heat; stir in dates and soda (mixture will froth up). Stand for 15 minutes or until dates are softened. Transfer mixture to a food processor; pulse until coarsely chopped.
3 Beat butter and sugar in a medium bowl with an electric mixer for 6 minutes or until pale and fluffy. Beat in eggs, one at a time, until well combined. Add combined sifted flour and baking powder alternately with combined milk and extract, beginning and ending with flour; beat until just combined. Fold date mixture into cake mixture. Spoon mixture into pan.
4 Bake cake for 1 hour 25 minutes or until a skewer inserted into the centre comes out clean (you may need to cover the cake with baking paper for the last 20 minutes to prevent it from overbrowning). Stand cake in pan for 10 minutes before turning, top-side up, onto a wire rack to cool.
5 Make cream cheese frosting.
6 Spread cream cheese frosting over cake.

CREAM CHEESE FROSTING Beat ingredients in a small bowl with an electric mixer for 6 minutes or until smooth.

TIP Don't be too concerned if your cake has a small dip in the middle; it will be covered with icing.
TECHNIQUES Step 1: see *'lining a square cake pan'*, page 276.
DO-AHEAD The cake can be made a day ahead; store in an airtight container at room temperature.

INDULGENT CAKES

Flowers
& SYRUPS

FRAGRANT
INFUSIONS OF

flowers
and syrups
drench
unassuming
Cakes

IN SWEET NECTAR

Earl grey meringue
WITH SYRUP-SOAKED FIGS

PREP + COOK TIME **1 HOUR (+ COOLING)** SERVES **8**

2 earl grey tea bags
1 cup (220g) caster (superfine) sugar
4 egg whites, at room temperature
3 teaspoons cornflour (cornstarch)
1 teaspoon white vinegar
2 tablespoons pistachios, chopped

SYRUP-SOAKED FIGS
2 earl grey tea bags
4 long strips orange rind
1 cup (220g) caster (superfine) sugar
$^1/_2$ cup (125ml) water
$^1/_4$ cup (60ml) fresh orange juice
8 medium figs (480g), torn in half

SWEETENED MASCARPONE
500g (1 pound) mascarpone
1 teaspoon vanilla extract
1 tablespoon icing (confectioners') sugar

1 Preheat oven to 150°C/300°F. Grease a large oven tray. Mark an 18cm x 30cm (7$^1/_4$-inch x 12-inch) rectangle on a piece of baking paper; turn paper, marked-side down, onto tray.
2 Remove tea from bags; process with sugar until finely ground.
3 Beat egg whites in a medium bowl with an electric mixer until soft peaks form. Gradually add tea sugar mixture; beat until stiff and glossy. Sift cornflour over egg white mixture, add vinegar; fold in using a metal spoon. Spread mixture just inside marked rectangle on tray.

4 Reduce oven to 120°C/250°F; bake meringue for 45 minutes or until firm to the touch. Turn oven off; cool in oven with door ajar, for at least 4 hours or overnight. (The top will crack a little but don't worry it will be covered with cream.)
5 Before serving (about 30 minutes), make syrup-soaked figs, then sweetened mascarpone.
6 Just before serving, spread sweetened mascarpone on meringue. Top with figs; spoon syrup over figs. Sprinkle with pistachios.

SYRUP-SOAKED FIGS Stir tea bags, rind, sugar, the water and juice in a medium saucepan over medium heat until sugar dissolves. Bring to the boil; cook for 6 minutes or until syrup thickens slightly. Place figs in a large bowl. Strain syrup over figs, gently stir to combine. Cool.

SWEETENED MASCARPONE Beat ingredients in a medium bowl with an electric mixer until soft peaks form.

TIPS Room temperature egg whites will beat better than cold ones. It is also a good idea when separating eggs, to do one egg at a time over a small bowl, adding to the mixer one by one; that way if you break a yolk you won't spoil the whole batch.
DO-AHEAD The meringue can be made a day ahead; store in an airtight container at room temperature. Assemble just before serving.

Rosewater SPONGE WITH strawberry compote

PREP + COOK TIME 1 HOUR (+ COOLING) SERVES 12

1¹/₃ cups (200g) plain (all-purpose) flour
6 eggs
²/₃ cup (150g) caster (superfine) sugar
2 teaspoons rosewater
80g (2¹/₂ ounces) butter, melted
³/₄ cup (180ml) pouring cream
1 tablespoon icing (confectioners') sugar
1 teaspoon vanilla extract
20 unsprayed pink rose petals

STRAWBERRY COMPOTE
375g (12 ounces) strawberries, chopped roughly
¹/₃ cup (75g) caster (superfine) sugar
1¹/₂ tablespoons rosewater

1 Make strawberry compote.
2 Preheat oven to 180°C/350°F. Grease two 15cm (6-inch) round cake pans; line base and side with baking paper.
3 Sift half the flour three times into a small bowl. Repeat with remaining flour in another small bowl.
4 Beat 3 eggs, half the caster sugar and half the rosewater in a small bowl with an electric mixer until thick, pale and tripled in volume. Sift one bowl of sifted flour over egg mixture; using a large metal spoon, fold flour through egg mixture. Fold in half the melted butter. Divide mixture between pans.

5 Bake cakes for 15 minutes, swapping pans from top to bottom, halfway through cooking time, or until cake pulls away from the side of the pan slightly. Stand cakes in pans for 5 minutes before turning, top-side down, onto lightly greased baking-paper-covered wire racks to cool.
6 Wash and dry cake pans; grease then line base and side. Repeat steps 3, 4 and 5 with remaining flour, eggs, caster sugar, rosewater and butter. You need four cakes in total.
7 Beat cream, sifted icing sugar and extract in a small bowl with an electric mixer until soft peaks form.
8 Place one cake on a plate; spread with one-third of the compote and one-third of the cream. Repeat layering with remaining cakes, compote and cream, finishing with a cake. Decorate with rose petals; dust with a little extra icing sugar.

STRAWBERRY COMPOTE Place ingredients in a medium saucepan; bring to the boil. Cook, stirring occasionally, over medium heat, for 10 minutes or until strawberries soften and liquid is syrupy. Cool.

TIPS If you like, you can insert skewers into the cake to hold the layers in place while slicing. Cut through the top two cake layers and serve as a portion; cut through the bottom two cake layers as a second portion.
TECHNIQUES Step 2: see *'lining a round cake pan'*, page 276.
DO-AHEAD This cake is best made on day of serving.

Lavender fillo
MILLE FEUILLE

PREP + COOK TIME **1 HOUR 20 MINUTES (+ COOLING)** SERVES **8**

18 sheets fillo pastry
100g (3¹/₂ ounces) salt-reduced butter, melted
¹/₄ cup (35g) caster (superfine) sugar
2 teaspoons icing (confectioners') sugar

LAVENDER CUSTARD
3 cups (750ml) milk
8 egg yolks
1 cup (220g) caster (superfine) sugar
¹/₂ cup (75g) cornflour (cornstarch)
1¹/₂ tablespoons dried lavender flowers
¹/₂ cup (125ml) thickened (heavy) cream

1 Make lavender custard.
2 Preheat oven to 160°C/325°F. Grease three large oven trays; line with baking paper.
3 Brush a sheet of fillo with some of the melted butter; scatter with scant ³/₄ teaspoon of caster sugar. Repeat layering five times to form a six layer stack. Using a sharp knife and ruler as a guide, cut stack into two 12cm x 28cm (4³/₄-inch x 11¹/₄-inch) rectangles; discard trimmings.
4 Repeat step 3 two more times. You will have six equally-sized fillo stacks in total.
5 Place two fillo stacks, side by side, on each oven tray; cover with a sheet of baking paper. Stack trays on top of each other. Place a fourth oven tray on top of the stack; weight with an ovenproof dish (see TECHNIQUES).

6 Bake stacked trays for 15 minutes. Carefully remove from oven; remove dish, un-stack trays. Return trays to oven, on separate shelves; bake, uncovered, a further 10 minutes or until golden. (For even cooking, rotate trays during cooking. If pastry starts to puff, press it down with a spatula.) Cool pastry on trays. Transfer to an airtight container until ready to assemble.
7 To assemble mille feuille, place a fillo rectangle on a platter; spread with one-fifth of the lavender custard. Repeat layering, finishing with a fillo rectangle. Dust with icing sugar and decorate with lavender flowers, if you like.

LAVENDER CUSTARD Heat milk in a medium saucepan until almost boiling. Meanwhile, whisk egg yolks, sugar, cornflour and lavender flowers in a large bowl; gradually whisk in hot milk. Return mixture to pan; whisk continuously over medium heat for 7 minutes or until mixture boils and thickens. Remove from heat; continue to whisk a further minute. Strain into a medium bowl, cover surface with plastic wrap; refrigerate until cool. Just before using, beat cream in a small bowl with an electric mixer until soft peaks form; fold into lavender custard.

TIPS There are usually 22 sheets of pastry in a 375g (12-ounce) packet of fillo pastry. Dried lavender flowers are available from spice shops and online.
TECHNIQUES Step 5: see *'cooking fillo so it stays flat'*, page 276.
DO-AHEAD This recipe is best made on day of serving.

SYRUP CAKES

The rule of thumb with syrup cakes, is that either the cake is hot or the syrup. This is to ensure that the syrup adequately soaks into the cake. For dense cakes, pierce them first with a skewer to speed absorption.

LAVENDER

WHILE THEORETICALLY ALL VARIETIES OF LAVENDER ARE EDIBLE, ENGLISH LAVENDER (LAVENDER AUGUSTIFOLIA) IS CONSIDERED THE CULINARY TYPE, PRIZED FOR ITS SCENT AND SWEETER TASTE. EVEN SO, IT STILL HAS A VERY DEFINING CAMPHOR-LIKE TASTE, MEANING A LITTLE GOES A LONG WAY IN COOKING. TO DRY YOUR OWN, SIMPLY HANG BUNCHES OF THE FLOWER SPIKES UPSIDE DOWN IN A COOL, AIRY SPOT. ONCE DRIED, RUB THE FLOWERS FROM THE STALK AND SEAL IN AN AIRTIGHT CONTAINER.

EDIBLE FLOWERS *Depending on the season you will find various edible flowers such as violets, viola, roses, calendula, geraniums, borage flowers and nasturtiums, at larger greengrocers and grower's markets. Be wary of buying from a florist though, as most commercially grown flowers are sprayed with pesticides.*

FLOWER *Waters*

Flower waters are produced by distillation and in the case of rosewater it is a by-product of rose oil production. Bottles can be found in delis, Middle Eastern and Indian grocers with potency varying between brands. Also, keep in mind once opened the flavour can fade, therefore it's always an idea to sniff and taste test before using to gauge if you need more or less.

WHAT IS THAT

Cream of tartar is an acid in powder form which is available in the baking section of supermarkets. We've used it in some of our meringue recipes to create more aerated and stable beaten egg whites. You can still make the recipe without it.

Stiff & GLOSSY

In our meringue recipes we instruct 'to beat egg whites and sugar until stiff and glossy'. When sugar has dissolved in the whites the visual clue is its glossy appearance; rub a little of the mixture between your fingertips, it should feel smooth, not gritty. The beating process will take around 8 minutes. For best results and the greatest volume, beat the whites in a tall, small bowl so the beaters are well down in the mixture.

ELDERFLOWER

WHILE NOT NATIVE TO BRITAIN, THE WHITE-FLOWERING ELDER IS A COMMON SIGHT IN SUMMER, ALONG THE HEDGEROWS OF THE ENGLISH COUNTRYSIDE, WHERE FLOWERS ARE HARVESTED AND USED IN WINES, LIQUEURS AND CORDIAL SYRUPS. THE TASTE IS BOTH FLORAL AND REFRESHING, AND NOT TOO CLOYING. THE CORDIAL, WHICH IS WHAT WE'VE USED FOR OUR RECIPES, IS FOUND IN SUPERMARKETS AND DELIS.

SUBSTITUTES *While flower waters each have a unique taste that can't be replicated by another flavour, most of the cakes in this section could easily be flavoured with a little finely grated lemon or orange rind, or that universal of flavourings, vanilla.*

HOW TO LEVEL CAKE BATTER

For thick cake batters, use an offset spatula, or a cranked spatula as it is also known. These have a step in the blade, which allows it to be held level to the batter. For aerated cakes, such as sponges, it is better to spin the pan on the work surface, as too much handling can decrease the volume.

MAGICAL EGG WHITES

It is the egg white that provides volume to cakes. For meringues, separate eggs, one at a time to ensure no yolk contaminates the white, as the tiniest fleck will decrease aeration. As you whisk an egg white, the air bubbles pull the protein of the white onto the whisk to form a solid structure (what we call stiff peaks), however whisk too much beyond that without sugar and the whites start to break down.

Basil, lime and
STRAWBERRY CHEESECAKE

PREP + COOK TIME 1 HOUR (+ REFRIGERATION) SERVES 8

cooking oil spray

125g (4 ounces) scotch finger biscuits

75g (2½ ounces) butter, melted

3 teaspoons powdered gelatine

¼ cup (60ml) water

375g (12 ounces) cream cheese, softened

½ cup (110g) caster (superfine) sugar

1 tablespoon finely grated lime rind

300ml thickened (heavy) cream

½ cup (125ml) lime juice

2 tablespoons finely chopped fresh basil

2 tablespoons baby fresh basil leaves

BASIL-INFUSED STRAWBERRIES

2 tablespoons water

½ cup (160g) strawberry jam

1 tablespoon lime juice

8 large fresh basil leaves

250g (8 ounces) strawberries, halved

1 Spray a 20cm (8-inch) springform pan with cooking oil (don't use butter as this hardens in the fridge); line base with baking paper.

2 Process biscuits until fine. Add butter; process until combined. Press mixture firmly over base of pan. Refrigerate 30 minutes.

3 Sprinkle gelatine over the water in a small heatproof jug; stand jug in a small saucepan of simmering water, stir until gelatine dissolves. Cool. (See TECHNIQUES.)

4 Beat cream cheese, sugar and rind in a medium bowl with an electric mixer until smooth. Add cream; beat until smooth. Add juice, cooled gelatine mixture and finely chopped basil; beat until combined. Pour filling mixture over biscuit base. Cover; refrigerate for 3 hours or overnight until set.

5 Make basil-infused strawberries.

6 Just before serving, top cheesecake with strawberries and syrup; scatter with basil leaves.

BASIL-INFUSED STRAWBERRIES Stir the water, jam, juice and basil in a small saucepan over low heat until jam melts. Bring to the boil. Remove from heat; stir in strawberries. Cool. Discard basil.

TECHNIQUES Step 3: see also *'dissolving powdered gelatine'*, page 277.

DO-AHEAD The cheesecake can be made a day ahead; store, covered in the refrigerator.

Orange blossom and
RASPBERRY ANGEL FOOD CAKE

PREP + COOK TIME 50 MINUTES (+ COOLING) SERVES 12

Angel food cakes contain no fat. Their lightness comes from incorporating air into egg whites and an unusual cooking method. The cake mixture is placed in an ungreased pan with a tubular centre which makes it stick to the side, so don't use a pan with a non-stick coating. Once baked, it is inverted to keep the air suspended through the cake, otherwise it will sink like a soufflé.

125g (4 ounces) frozen raspberries, thawed
$1/2$ cup (75g) plain (all-purpose) flour
$1/2$ cup (75g) wheaten cornflour (cornstarch)
$1^1/_4$ cups (275g) caster (superfine) sugar
12 egg whites
1 teaspoon cream of tartar
2 teaspoons orange blossom water
$1/_4$ cup edible flowers

ORANGE BLOSSOM ICING
2 cups (320g) icing (confectioners') sugar
$1/_4$ teaspoon orange blossom water
$1/_4$ cup (60ml) strained lemon juice

1 Preheat oven to 180°C/350°F. Adjust oven shelf to lowest position.
2 Push raspberries through a fine sieve into a small bowl; discard seeds. Sift flours and $1/_4$ cup (55g) sugar together five times.
3 Beat egg whites in a large bowl with an electric mixer until foamy; beat in cream of tartar. Gradually add remaining sugar, beating until sugar dissolves and mixture is very thick and glossy. Whisk in orange blossom water. Sift one-third of the flour mixture on meringue; gently fold through using a balloon whisk. Repeat with remaining flour mixture, in batches.

4 Transfer one-third of the cake mixture to a medium bowl; fold in raspberry puree. Carefully fold raspberry mixture into remaining cake mixture, swirling to create a marbled effect. Spoon mixture into an ungreased 25cm (10-inch) angel food cake pan with a removal base; smooth surface.
5 Bake cake for 30 minutes or until cake springs back when pressed lightly with a finger.
6 Place a piece of baking paper, just larger than the pan on a work surface. Immediately turn hot pan upside-down on the paper; leave to cool completely in this position. The cake will drop when cold; if not, you may need to run a spatula around the cake to release it.
7 Make orange blossom icing.
8 Drizzle cooled cake with icing; decorate with flowers.

ORANGE BLOSSOM ICING Sift icing sugar into a small bowl; stir in orange blossom water and enough of the juice to form an icing the consistency of honey.

TIPS We used a Middle Eastern brand of orange blossom water with a pronounced flavour. Taste and adjust the icing with more if necessary. A balloon whisk has a large rounded end and soft flexible wires. If yours is tear-dropped shaped with stiff wires, you can still use it, just take care to use a gentle folding action. You could decorate the cake with 125g (4 ounces) fresh raspberries instead of the flowers.
DO-AHEAD The cake is best made on day of serving.

Lemon and earl grey chiffon syrup cake
[RECIPE PAGES 218 & 219]

Lemon and earl grey CHIFFON SYRUP CAKE

PREP + COOK TIME 1 HOUR 20 MINUTES (+ COOLING) SERVES 12

Chiffon cakes share cooking principles with angel food cakes. Both derive their lightness from a large quantity of whisked egg whites. However, a chiffon cake also includes egg yolks aerated with sugar, as well as a large amount of liquid and oil to provide a richer mouth feel. It is also cooked in an ungreased pan with a tubular centre with the intention that the cake sticks to the side. Once cooked, it is immediately inverted to keep the air suspended throughout the cake, otherwise it will sink like a soufflé.

2 cups (300g) self-raising flour
2 teaspoons french earl grey tea leaves
1$^1/_2$ cups (330g) caster (superfine) sugar
7 eggs, separated
$^3/_4$ cup (180ml) strained lemon juice
$^1/_2$ cup (125ml) extra virgin olive oil
1 tablespoon finely grated lemon rind
$^1/_2$ teaspoon cream of tartar
600ml thickened (heavy) cream
2 tablespoons borage flowers (optional)

EARL GREY TEA SYRUP
1 tablespoon french earl grey tea leaves
1 cup (250ml) boiling water
1 cup (220g) caster (superfine) sugar

1 Preheat oven to 180°C/350°F. Adjust oven shelf to lowest position, place an oven tray on the shelf.
2 Triple-sift flour into a medium bowl.
3 Process tea leaves and $^3/_4$ cup (165g) of the sugar until leaves are finely chopped. Transfer mixture to a small bowl of an electric mixer, add egg yolks; beat for 5 minutes or until thick and pale. Gradually add juice, oil and half the rind, beating until well combined. Transfer mixture to a large bowl; sift flour over mixture, then fold gently with a whisk until just incorporated.
4 Beat egg whites in a large bowl with an electric mixer until soft peaks form. Add cream of tartar, then gradually add remaining sugar, beating until mixture is thick and glossy. Fold egg white mixture into yolk mixture, in two batches, until just combined. Spoon mixture into an ungreased 25cm (10-inch) angel food cake pan with a removable base; smooth surface.
5 Place cake pan on preheated oven tray; bake for 50 minutes or until a skewer inserted into the centre comes out clean. Place a piece of baking paper, just larger than the pan on work surface. Immediately turn hot pan upside-down on the paper; leave to cool completely in this position.

[PHOTOGRAPH PAGES 216 & 217]

6 Meanwhile, make earl grey tea syrup.

7 Carefully run a small knife around the edge of cake and the tube to help release cake from pan (you may also need to run a knife or spatula between the base and the cake). Using a serrated knife, split cake in half horizontally.

8 Beat cream in a small bowl with an electric mixer until soft peaks form; fold in remaining rind. Place the base cake layer on a cake plate or stand; spread with a little more than half the cream. Finish with remaining cake layer and cream. Decorate with flowers; drizzle with syrup.

EARL GREY TEA SYRUP Combine tea leaves and the boiling water in a small saucepan; stand for 10 minutes. Add sugar; stir over low heat until sugar dissolves. Bring to the boil. Boil for 5 minutes or until syrup is reduced slightly. Cool. Strain.

TIPS French earl grey tea is similar to ordinary earl grey, except that it contains rose petals; lady grey tea contains additions of either lavender or seville orange. Any form of earl grey tea you prefer can be used.

VARIATION For an orange blosom and mint tea syrup cake, omit the french earl grey tea in the cake and instead add 1 tablespoon orange blossom water with the lemon juice in step 3. Omit the earl grey syrup and instead make 'orange blossom and mint tea syrup' on page 222. Serve the cake drizzled with syrup.

DO-AHEAD The cake and syrup can be made a day ahead, store in separate airtight containers at room temperature.

Lemon and earl grey
CHIFFON SYRUP CAKE

[RECIPE PAGES 218 & 219]

MAKING THE TEA SUGAR MIXTURE FOR THE CAKE

Process tea leaves and ¾ cup (165g) of the sugar until leaves are finely chopped. If you've got a small food processor bowl use this.

MAKING THE CAKE BATTER

Using a large metal spoon and a gentle lifting and folding action, add the egg white mixture to the egg yolk mixture, in two batches, folding only until just combined.

INVERTING THE COOKED CAKE

To prevent the cake from sinking, carefully invert the cooked cake in the pan over a piece of baking paper; leave to cool. The cake will be stuck to the side of the pan which will prevent it from falling out, while the air that has been trapped during baking will be forced back down through the cake keeping it aerated.

MAKING THE EARL GREY TEA SYRUP

Combine tea leaves and the boiling water in a small saucepan, leave to infuse for 10 minutes before adding the sugar and placing on the stove top to finish making the syrup.

SPLITTING THE CAKE

Using a ruler, mark the halfway mark on the cake at several points making slits. Holding a long serrated knife horizontally, use the markings as a guide to cut the cake in half.

SERVING

Assemble the cake on a platter, layering it with the cream. Drizzle the cake with earl grey tea syrup just before serving. Cut slices of cake using a finely serrated knife.

Passionfruit cake with orange
BLOSSOM AND MINT TEA SYRUP

PREP + COOK TIME 1 HOUR 45 MINUTES (+ STANDING & COOLING) SERVES 8

220g (7 ounces) unsalted butter, softened
1 cup (220g) caster (superfine) sugar
3 eggs
2 cups (300g) self-raising flour
$^2/_3$ cup (160ml) buttermilk
$^1/_3$ cup (80ml) passionfruit pulp
1 tablespoon edible flowers (optional)

ORANGE BLOSSOM AND MINT TEA SYRUP
1 peppermint tea bag
1 cup (250ml) boiling water
1 cup (220g) caster (superfine) sugar
$^1/_2$ cup (125ml) passionfruit pulp
1 teaspoon orange blossom water

1 Make orange blossom and mint tea syrup.
2 Preheat oven to 180°C/350°F. Grease a 12cm x 23cm ($4^3/_4$-inch x $9^1/_4$-inch) loaf pan; line base with baking paper.
3 Beat butter and sugar in a medium bowl with an electric mixer for 6 minutes or until pale and fluffy. Beat in eggs, one at a time. Fold in flour, then buttermilk in alternate batches; fold in passionfruit until just combined. Spoon mixture into pan; smooth surface.
4 Bake cake for 50 minutes or until a skewer inserted into the centre comes out clean. Stand cake in pan for 10 minutes before turning, top-side up, onto a wire rack to cool.
5 Place cake on a plate; spoon half the syrup over the cake. Decorate with flowers. Serve cake with remaining syrup.

ORANGE BLOSSOM AND MINT TEA SYRUP Place tea bag in a small saucepan, pour over boiling water; steep for 5 minutes. Squeeze liquid from tea bag; discard bag. Add sugar and passionfruit pulp to tea; stir over low heat until sugar dissolves. Increase heat to high; bring to the boil, boil for 15 minutes or until thick and syrupy. Remove from heat; stir in orange blossom water. Cool.

TIP You will need about 12 passionfruit for this recipe.
DO-AHEAD This cake is best made on day of serving.

Orange blossom trifle cake
[RECIPE PAGES 226 & 227]

Orange blossom
TRIFLE CAKE

PREP + COOK TIME 2 HOURS (+ REFRIGERATION & COOLING) SERVES 12

4 eggs
1/2 cup (110g) caster (superfine) sugar
2/3 cup (100g) plain (all-purpose) flour
60g (2 ounces) butter, melted
20g (3/4 ounce) flaked almonds
1/4 cup (60ml) orange juice
2 tablespoons golden syrup
1/4 cup (40g) icing (confectioners') sugar
1 teaspoon orange blossom water
4 medium oranges (1kg), segmented (see TECHNIQUES)
300ml thickened (heavy) cream

ORANGE JELLY

6 titanium-strength gelatine leaves (30g)
2 cups (500ml) strained fresh orange juice
2/3 cup (150g) caster (superfine) sugar
1 cup (250ml) dessert wine
red and yellow food colouring

CRÈME PÂTISSIÈRE

1 1/4 cups (310ml) milk
2 wide strips orange rind
3 egg yolks
1/4 cup (55g) caster (superfine) sugar
1 tablespoon plain (all-purpose) flour
1 1/2 tablespoon cornflour (cornstarch)

1 Make orange jelly, then crème pâtissière.
2 Preheat oven to 180°C/350°F. Grease a deep 22cm (9-inch) round cake pan; line base with baking paper.
3 Beat eggs and caster sugar in a small bowl with an electric mixer for 8 minutes or until thick and creamy. Transfer to a large bowl. Sift half the flour over egg mixture; carefully fold in flour. Sift remaining flour over mixture; fold into mixture. Working quickly, fold in butter. Pour mixture into pan.
4 Bake cake for 25 minutes or until the top springs back when touched lightly in the centre. Turn immediately, top-side down, onto a baking-paper-covered wire rack to cool.
5 Spread almonds in a single layer on an oven tray; roast for 6 minutes or until toasted lightly. Cool.
6 Combine juice, golden syrup, 1 tablespoon of the icing sugar and half the orange blossom water; brush over top and side of cake. Arrange orange segments on cake in circles. Whisk crème pâtissière smooth; spoon on oranges.
7 Beat cream, remaining icing sugar and remaining orange blossom water in a small bowl with an electric mixer until soft peaks form. Spread cream mixture on crème pâtissière.
8 Turn jelly onto a board covered with a sheet of baking paper; chop jelly into 2cm (3/4-inch) cubes. Just before serving, place jelly on cream; scatter with nuts.

ORANGE JELLY Soak gelatine leaves in a bowl of cold water for 5 minutes or until softened (see TECHNIQUES). Meanwhile, stir juice and sugar in a small saucepan until sugar dissolves; remove from heat. Squeeze excess water from gelatine, add to pan; stir until gelatine dissolves. Stir in wine. Tint mixture orange using a few drops of red and yellow food colouring. Pour into 20cm x 30cm (8-inch x 12-inch) slice pan. Refrigerate for 3 hours or overnight until set.

CRÈME PÂTISSIÈRE Heat milk and rind in a medium saucepan until mixture comes to a gentle simmer. Remove from heat; discard rind. Whisk egg yolks, sugar and flours in a medium bowl until combined. Gradually whisk hot milk into egg yolk mixture. Return mixture to cleaned pan; cook, stirring, over low heat until custard thickens enough to coat the back of a wooden spoon. Pour into a clean bowl; cover surface with plastic wrap. Cool to room temperature. Refrigerate until required.

TIPS You will need about 12 oranges for this recipe. Gelatine leaves, available from delicatessens and some supermarkets have a neutral taste and are easier to dissolve than powdered gelatine. If using powdered gelatine, use 2 tablespoons; scatter over warm sugar and juice mixture; stir until dissolved.

TECHNIQUES Step 1: see also *'dissolving gelatine leaves'*, page 277. Step 2: see *'lining a round cake pan'*, page 276. Step 6: see *'segmenting citrus'*, page 276.

DO-AHEAD The jelly and custard can be made 2 days ahead. The cake is best made and assembled on the day of serving.

[PHOTOGRAPH PAGES 224 & 225]

Orange blossom TRIFLE CAKE

[RECIPE PAGES 226 & 227]

MAKING THE ORANGE JELLY

Squeeze excess water from the gelatine leaves and add to the hot juice and sugar mixture; stir until dissolved. Stir in wine and tint mixture with food colouring.

MAKING THE CRÈME PÂTISSIÈRE

Whisk egg yolks, sugar and flour in a medium bowl until combined and smooth. While whisking continuously, gradually pour hot milk mixture onto egg yolk mixture, until combined.

ADDING BUTTER TO SPONGE MIXTURE

After you've added flour to the egg yolk and sugar mixture, gently fold in the butter. Use a light hand so you don't deflate the batter.

STARTING TO ASSEMBLE THE CAKE

Once you've brushed the cake with the syrup mixture, place the orange segments in concentric circles with the wider part of each segment facing outwards.

ADDING THE CRÈME PÂTISSIÈRE AND CREAM LAYERS

Spoon a layer of crème pâtissière onto the orange segments. Gently spoon the cream mixture over the crème pâtissière layer, peaking it as you go. Decorate the top with jelly cubes, flaked almonds and edible flowers.

SERVING

The trifle is easy to serve, however because of the lovely moist layers it doesn't cut neatly; it really is a trifle. Cut slices and place in cups or wide bowls scooping up any fallen pieces of topping.

Rose and almond SYRUP CAKE

PREP + COOK TIME 1 HOUR SERVES 4

1¼ cups (150g) ground almonds
¼ cup (15g) fresh white breadcrumbs
1 teaspoon baking powder
3 eggs, separated
¾ cup (165g) caster (superfine) sugar
3 teaspoons rosewater
¼ cup (60ml) pouring cream
1½ tablespoons slivered almonds
2 tablespoons pistachios, halved
1 tablespoon slivered almonds, roasted, extra

SYRUP
¾ cup (165g) caster (superfine) sugar
1 cup (250ml) water
2 tablespoons dried rose buds

1 Preheat oven 180°C/350°F. Grease an 18cm (7¼-inch) heart-shaped cake pan; line base and side with baking paper.
2 Combine ground almonds, breadcrumbs and baking powder in a medium bowl. Beat egg yolks and sugar in a small bowl with an electric mixer until creamy. Beat in rosewater and cream until just combined; stir in breadcrumb mixture.
3 Beat egg whites in a small bowl with an electric mixer until soft peaks form. Fold egg whites into almond mixture, in two batches. Pour mixture into pan; top with half the almonds.
4 Bake cake for 45 minutes or until a skewer inserted into the centre comes out clean. Cake will have a slight dip in it.
5 Meanwhile, make syrup.
6 Stand cake in pan for 5 minutes; pour half the hot syrup over the cake. Cool.
7 Turn cake, top-side up onto a plate. Scatter with pistachios and extra roasted almonds. Serve with remaining syrup.

SYRUP Stir sugar and water in a small saucepan over medium heat until sugar dissolves. Bring to the boil; simmer for 3 minutes. Stir in rose buds. Cool for 10 minutes to infuse flavours.

TIP You could also make this cake in a deep 18cm (7¼-inch) round cake pan.
DO-AHEAD This cake is best made on day of serving.

Turkish delight roulade with pomegranate syrup
[RECIPE PAGES 234 & 235]

Turkish delight roulade
WITH POMEGRANATE SYRUP

PREP + COOK TIME 1 HOUR (+ REFRIGERATION & COOLING) SERVES 8

4 eggs, separated

1/2 cup (110g) caster (superfine) sugar

40g (1 1/2 ounces) butter, melted

2 tablespoons hot water

1 teaspoon vanilla extract

1/2 cup (75g) self-raising flour

2 tablespoons caster (superfine) sugar, extra

15g (1/2 ounce) rose persian fairy floss (optional)

JELLY

2 medium pomegranates (640g)

3 titanium-strength gelatine leaves (15g)

1 cup (250ml) rosé wine

1 cup (220g) caster (superfine) sugar

2 teaspoons rosewater

FILLING

250g (4 ounces) mascarpone

1/3 cup (80ml) thickened (heavy) cream

1 Make jelly, then filling.

2 Preheat oven 180°C/350°F. Grease 26cm x 32cm (10 1/2-inch x 12 3/4-inch) swiss roll pan; line base and long sides with baking paper extending the paper 2cm (3/4 inch) above sides.

3 Beat egg yolks and sugar in a small bowl with an electric mixer for 5 minutes or until thick and pale. Add combined butter, water and extract; fold in sifted flour. Beat egg whites in a large bowl with an electric mixer until soft peaks form; fold into flour mixture, in two batches. Pour mixture into pan; smooth surface.

4 Bake cake for 12 minutes or until just firm to the touch. Turn cake onto a large piece of baking paper, sprinkled with extra sugar; trim edges of cake slightly. Using paper as a guide, roll up hot cake from a long side; stand for 2 minutes. Unroll; cool.

5 Spread cake with filling, leaving a 1cm (1/2-inch) border on all sides. Place half the jelly cubes in one line across cream. Using paper as a guide, roll up the cake. Place roulade on a tray; refrigerate for 3 hours or until firm.

6 Just before serving, drizzle roulade with chilled syrup; top with reserved pomegranate seeds, remaining jelly and fairy floss.

JELLY Remove seeds from pomegranate (see TECHNIQUES); reserve $^{1}/_{3}$ cup seeds. Process remaining seeds to a rough puree; strain. You need $^{1}/_{2}$ cup (125ml) juice. Soak gelatine in a large bowl of cold water 4 minutes or until softened (see TECHNIQUES). Stir wine and sugar in a medium saucepan over medium heat until sugar dissolves. Bring to the boil; simmer for 1 minute. Add pomegranate juice and rosewater; bring almost to the boil. Transfer 1 cup (250ml) mixture to a small bowl. Squeeze excess water from gelatine, add to bowl; stir until gelatine dissolves. Pour into a small container so jelly is 2cm ($^{3}/_{4}$-inch) deep. Refrigerate for 3 hours or until set. Unmould jelly; cut into 2cm ($^{3}/_{4}$-inch) cubes. Meanwhile, simmer remaining syrup in pan for 5 minutes or until thickened slightly. Refrigerate until needed.

FILLING Beat ingredients with 2 tablespoons of the chilled syrup in a bowl with an electric mixer until soft peaks form. Refrigerate.

TIPS Persian fairy floss, also known as pashmak, is available from delicatessens and gourmet food stores in assorted flavours. We used a 3 cup plastic takeaway container to mould the jelly. You can substitute 2 teaspoons powdered gelatine for gelatine leaves in the jelly. Place $^{1}/_{4}$ cup (60ml) jelly mixture in a small heatproof cup, sprinkle over powdered gelatine. Place cup in a saucepan filled with a shallow amount of simmering water; stir until gelatine dissolves. Combine gelatine mixture with remaining jelly mixture and set as instructed.

TECHNIQUES Step 1: see *'removing seeds from a pomegranate'*, page 276 and *'dissolving gelatine leaves'*, page 277.

DO-AHEAD The jelly can be made a day ahead. The cake is best made and assembled on day of serving.

[PHOTOGRAPH PAGES 232 & 233]

Cinnamon sponge with
RASPBERRIES AND LAVENDER SUGAR

PREP + COOK TIME 1 HOUR (+ STANDING & COOLING) SERVES 6

³/₄ cup (110g) plain (all-purpose) flour

¹/₂ cup (75g) cornflour (cornstarch)

2 teaspoons ground cinnamon

6 eggs

³/₄ cup (165g) caster (superfine) sugar

50g (1¹/₂ ounces) unsalted butter, melted, cooled

1¹/₂ cups (375ml) thickened (heavy) cream

¹/₂ cup (160g) raspberry jam

250g (8 ounces) raspberries

LAVENDER SUGAR

¹/₂ cup (110g) caster (superfine) sugar

4 fresh lavender flowers (or 1 teaspoon dried lavender)

1 Make lavender sugar.

2 Preheat oven to 180°C/350°F. Grease two 20cm (8-inch) round cake pans; line bases with baking paper.

3 Sift flours and cinnamon together three times.

4 Beat eggs and sugar in a large bowl with an electric mixer for 8 minutes or until thick, pale and tripled in volume. Sift one-third of the flour mixture over egg mixture; gently fold in with a large metal spoon. Repeat with remaining flour mixture, in two batches.

5 Transfer a quarter of the cake mixture to a small bowl; fold in melted butter. Carefully fold butter mixture back into remaining cake mixture. Divide mixture between pans.

6 Bake cakes for 25 minutes, rotating pans on shelf, or until cakes spring back when pressed lightly with your finger and come away from the side of the pan. Immediately, turn top-side down, onto baking-paper-covered wire racks. Cool.

7 Beat cream in a small bowl with an electric mixer until soft peaks form. Place one cake on a plate; spread with jam, then half the cream. Finish with second cake and remaining cream. Decorate with three-quarter of the raspberries; sprinkle with lavender sugar. Serve cake with remaining raspberries.

LAVENDER SUGAR Place sugar and lavender in a jar; leave for at least 4 hours or overnight for lavender scent to infuse sugar.

TIP Dried lavender is available from selected delis and spice shops. If you prefer, you can use 1 teaspoon finely grated orange or lemon rind instead.

TECHNIQUES Step 2: see *'lining a round cake pan'*, page 276.

DO-AHEAD The lavender sugar can be made up to 6 weeks ahead. The sponge is best made on day of serving.

Lime and yoghurt cakes
WITH ELDERFLOWER SYRUP

PREP + COOK TIME **1 HOUR 20 MINUTES** MAKES **8**

250g (8 ounces) butter, softened
2 teaspoons vanilla extract
1 tablespoon finely grated lime rind
1 cup (220g) caster (superfine) sugar
3 eggs, separated
2 cups (300g) self-raising flour
1 cup (280g) Greek-style yoghurt
2 tablespoons edible white flowers (optional)

CANDIED LIME RIND
3 limes
$1/2$ cup (110g) caster (superfine) sugar
1 cup (250ml) water
$1/4$ cup (55g) caster (superfine) sugar, extra

ELDERFLOWER SYRUP
$1/3$ cup (80ml) strained lime juice
$3/4$ cup (165g) caster (superfine) sugar
$1/4$ cup (60ml) water
$1/2$ cup (125ml) elderflower cordial

1 Make candied lime rind.
2 Preheat oven to 180°C/350°F. Grease eight 11cm ($4^1/2$-inch) mini kugelhopf pans.
3 Beat butter, extract, rind and sugar in a small bowl with an electric mixer until pale and fluffy. Beat in egg yolks, one at a time, until just combined. Transfer mixture to a large bowl; fold in sifted flour and yoghurt, in two batches.

4 Beat egg whites in a small bowl with an electric mixer until soft peaks form; fold into cake mixture, in two batches. Spoon mixture into pans; smooth surface.
5 Bake cakes for 30 minutes or until a skewer inserted into the centre comes out clean. Stand cakes in pans for 5 minutes before turning out onto a wire rack placed over an oven tray.
6 Meanwhile, make elderflower syrup.
7 Pour hot syrup evenly over hot cakes. Serve cakes warm or cool, topped with candied rind, remaining syrup and flowers.

CANDIED LIME RIND Peel rind from limes into 1cm ($1/2$-inch) wide strips; place rind in a small saucepan, cover with water. Bring to the boil; drain. Repeat four times. Return rind to pan with sugar and the water; simmer, uncovered, for 20 minutes or until rind is translucent and most of the syrup has evaporated. Drain. Place candied rind on a wire rack to cool. Toss rind in extra sugar to coat. Cut into shorter lengths.

ELDERFLOWER SYRUP Heat ingredients in a small saucepan over low heat, without boiling, until sugar dissolves. Bring to the boil; remove from heat.

TIP Mini kugelhopf pans, also known as bundt pans, are sold in packs of two from leading department and kitchenware shops.
DO-AHEAD The candied lime rind can be made a day ahead; store in an airtight container. The cakes are best made on day of serving.

Watermelon, rose and STRAWBERRY ALMOND CAKE

PREP + COOK TIME 1 HOUR (+ COOLING) SERVES 12

1 cup (160g) blanched almonds
³/₄ cup (165g) caster (superfine) sugar
¹/₄ teaspoon sea salt flakes
5 egg whites
2 teaspoons vanilla bean paste
375g (12 ounces) mascarpone
200g (8 ounces) sour cream
2 teaspoons rosewater
200g (6¹/₂ ounces) strawberries, sliced

CANDIED WATERMELON
2.5kg (5-pound) wedge seedless watermelon
1¹/₂ cups (330g) caster (superfine) sugar
³/₄ cup (180ml) water
¹/₄ cup (60ml) lime juice

1 Preheat oven to 180°C/350°F. Grease a shallow 28cm x 33cm (11¹/₄-inch x 13¹/₄-inch) swiss roll pan; line with baking paper.
2 Process almonds, ¹/₄ cup (55g) caster sugar and salt until fine.
3 Beat egg whites in a large bowl with an electric mixer until soft peaks form. Gradually add remaining sugar, beating until mixture is thick and glossy and sugar is dissolved. Using a large metal spoon, fold almond mixture and vanilla paste into meringue until just incorporated. Spoon mixture into pan; smooth surface.
4 Bake cake for 20 minutes or until golden and firm to the touch. Cool in pan.
5 Meanwhile, make candied watermelon.

6 Beat ¹/₂ cup (125ml) reserved watermelon syrup with mascarpone, sour cream and rosewater in a medium bowl with an electric mixer until soft peaks form.
7 Turn cake, top-side up, onto a chopping board; cut crossways into three rectangles. Place one cake rectangle on a platter; spread with one-third of the cream, top with enough candied watermelon pieces to cover cream in a single layer, trimming and adding as necessary. Top with another cake rectangle, half the remaining cream and remaining watermelon pieces. Finish layering with last cake rectangle and remaining cream. Decorate with strawberries and candied watermelon cubes.

CANDIED WATERMELON Trim rind from watermelon. Cut watermelon lengthways into 1.5cm (³/₄-inch) slices. Trim slices into 6cm x 23cm (2¹/₂-inch x 9¹/₄-inch) rectangles; cut in half crossways. Cut trimmings into 1.5cm (³/₄-inch) cubes. Place sugar and water in a 28cm (11¹/₄-inch) frying pan over medium heat; stir until sugar dissolves and mixture boils. Stir in juice. Cook large watermelon pieces in syrup, in three batches, for 3 minutes each side. Using a slotted spoon, transfer pieces to a paper-towel-lined tray. Cook watermelon cubes in same syrup for 6 minutes; transfer to tray. Pour syrup into a small bowl; cool, adding any more syrup that drains from the watermelon to it. Reserve syrup.

DO-AHEAD The almond cake can be made a day ahead; store in an airtight container at room temperature.

Apples
& PEARS

AUTUMNAL

Apples and pears

BRING

Fruity flavour

IN FROM THE ORCHARD

Plum and lemon POLENTA CAKE

PREP + COOK TIME **1 HOUR 40 MINUTES (+ COOLING)** SERVES 8

2/3 cup (110g) dry-roasted almonds

1 1/3 cups (100g) shredded coconut

3/4 cup (125g) fine polenta

1 teaspoon baking powder

225g (8 ounces) salt-reduced butter, softened, chopped

1 cup (220g) caster (superfine) sugar

1 tablespoon finely grated lemon rind

4 eggs

1/4 cup (60ml) limoncello

2 teaspoons icing (confectioners') sugar

VANILLA-POACHED PLUMS

16 small ripe plums (1.2kg), halved, stones removed, each half cut into three wedges

1/2 cup (110g) caster (superfine) sugar

2 teaspoons finely grated lemon rind

1/2 teaspoon vanilla extract

1 Make vanilla-poached plums.

2 Preheat oven to 170°C/340°F. Grease a 22cm (9-inch) springform pan; line base and side with baking paper.

3 Process almonds until finely ground. Combine ground almonds with coconut, polenta and baking powder in a medium bowl.

4 Beat butter, sugar and rind in a medium bowl with an electric mixer until pale and fluffy. Beat in eggs, one at a time, until well combined. Fold in combined dry ingredients until mixture just starts to come together. Add limoncello; mix until just combined. Spread half the cake mixture into pan.

5 Drain 450g (14 1/2 ounces) of the vanilla-poached plums; arrange plums evenly on cake mixture. Dollop remaining cake mixture over plums then gently spread to cover plums.

6 Bake cake for 1 1/4 hours or until a skewer inserted into the centre comes out clean. Stand cake in pan 15 minutes before transferring to a wire rack to cool.

7 Place cake on plate; dust with icing sugar. Top cake with remaining plums and syrup.

VANILLA-POACHED PLUMS Place ingredients in a medium heavy-based saucepan over low heat; cook, covered, shaking pan occasionally, for 10 minutes or until plums start to soften and release juice. Remove lid; cook a further 7 minutes, shaking pan occasionally, or until syrup reduces and thickens slightly. Cool.

TIPS You may need to cover the cake with baking paper for the last 10 minutes of cooking time to prevent over browning. Use a melon baller to remove plum stones with ease and avoid bruising the fruit. Limencello is an Italian lemon liqueur from liquor stores; you could use white rum instead.

TECHNIQUES Step 2: see *'lining a round cake pan'*, page 276.

DO-AHEAD Plums can be poached a day ahead; keep refrigerated. This cake is best made on day of serving.

Spiced apple stack cake

PREP + COOK TIME 3 HOURS (+ REFRIGERATION) SERVES 16

You will need to start this recipe the day before.

600g (1$^1/_4$ pounds) dried apple slices
1.5 litres (6 cups) water
1 cup (220g) firmly packed brown sugar
2 teaspoons ground cinnamon
$^1/_2$ teaspoon ground nutmeg
$^1/_2$ teaspoon ground allspice
$^1/_4$ teaspoon ground cloves
250g (8 ounces) butter, softened
2 cups (440g) caster (superfine) sugar
2 teaspoons vanilla extract
2 eggs
2 cups (300g) plain (all-purpose) flour
4 cups (600g) self-raising flour
1 teaspoon bicarbonate of soda (baking soda)
$^1/_4$ teaspoon salt
$^2/_3$ cup (160ml) buttermilk
1$^1/_2$ tablespoons icing (confectioners') sugar
3 cinnamon sticks

1 Place apples and the water in a large saucepan; cover surface with a round of baking paper, then a small plate to weight down. Bring to the boil over high heat. Reduce heat; simmer, for 20 minutes or until apple is soft. Drain. Cool. Blend or process apple, in batches, until smooth; transfer to a large bowl. Stir in brown sugar and spices.
2 Preheat oven to 180°C/350°F. Grease and line two oven trays with baking paper.

3 Beat butter, caster sugar and extract in a small bowl with an electric mixer until pale and fluffy. Beat in eggs, one at a time, until just combined. Transfer mixture to a large bowl. Sift flours, soda and salt into another large bowl. Stir flour mixture into creamed mixture alternately with buttermilk, in three batches, until combined (mixture will be stiff; you may need to finish combining with your hands). Knead dough on a floured surface until smooth and combined.
4 Divide dough into eight equal portions. Roll one portion of dough between sheets of baking paper into a 23cm (9$^1/_4$-inch) round. Using a 22cm (9-inch) plate or cake pan as a guide, cut round from dough. Transfer to one tray. Repeat with another portion of dough and second tray.
5 Bake for 12 minutes, swapping trays from top to bottom halfway through cooking time or until golden. Stand dough on trays for 5 minutes before transferring to wire racks to cool. Repeat steps 4 and 5 with remaining dough portions, in batches, to make eight rounds in total.
6 Place a cake round on a platter or cake stand; spread with a slightly rounded $^1/_2$ cup of apple filling. Repeat layering with remaining cake rounds and apple filling, finishing with a cake round. Cover cake with plastic wrap; refrigerate overnight. Just before serving, dust cake with icing sugar; decorate with cinnamon sticks.

DO-AHEAD This cake needs to be made at least a day ahead. Or, up to 2 days ahead; store, covered, in the refrigerator.

Spiced apple stack cake

[RECIPE PAGE 249]

MAKING THE ROUND OF BAKING PAPER
Fold a square of baking paper into quarters. Fold the square in half on the diagonal, then in half again to form a thin triangle. Hold the tip of the triangle over the centre of the pan; trim any paper that extends over the rim. Open out the folded paper.

ADDING SPICES TO THE COOKED APPLES
Stir spices into the pureed cooked apples; refrigerate until needed.

MAKING THE CAKE DOUGH
Stir the flour mixture into the creamed mixture alternately with the buttermilk, in three batches. You will need to work quite vigorously to incorporate the last batch of flour and don't be afraid to use your hands, if your arms get tired.

ROLLING THE DOUGH FOR THE CAKE LAYERS

Roll portions of dough, one at a time, with a floured rolling pin on floured baking paper or between sheets of baking paper until dough is about 23cm (9¼ inches) round.

TRIMMING THE CAKE INTO ROUNDS

Place a 22cm (9-inch) upturned plate or bowl on the round of dough. Using the tip of a small knife, gently cut the dough following the edge of the plate as a guide; discard dough scraps. Repeat trimming with each rolled out dough round.

SERVING

Allow about 20 minutes to layer the cake rounds and filling. Just before serving, dust the top with icing sugar. The cake cuts easily with a long thin bladed knife. Serve with cream or ice-cream.

Eggnog apple cake
WITH BROWN BUTTER FROSTING

PREP + COOK TIME 2 HOURS (+ COOLING) SERVES 10

4 small green apples (520g), peeled, chopped finely

$^{1}/_{4}$ cup (60ml) brandy

$^{1}/_{4}$ cup (55g) caster (superfine) sugar

170g (5$^{1}/_{2}$ ounces) butter, softened

80g (2$^{1}/_{2}$ ounces) cream cheese, softened

1$^{1}/_{4}$ cups (275g) caster (superfine) sugar, extra

2 teaspoons vanilla extract

4 eggs

1$^{1}/_{2}$ cups (225g) plain (all-purpose) flour

1 teaspoon baking powder

1 teaspoon ground nutmeg

$^{1}/_{2}$ teaspoon salt

$^{1}/_{4}$ teaspoon ground nutmeg, extra

BROWN BUTTER FROSTING

80g (2$^{1}/_{2}$ ounces) butter

125g (4 ounces) butter, extra, softened

1$^{1}/_{2}$ cups (350g) icing (confectioners') sugar

1 teaspoon vanilla extract

1 Preheat oven to 160°C/325°F. Grease a 20cm (8-inch) round cake pan; line base and side with baking paper.

2 Combine apple, brandy and sugar in a large saucepan; cook, stirring, over medium heat until sugar dissolves. Reduce heat to low; cook, uncovered, stirring occasionally, for 10 minutes or until apple is tender. Cool.

3 Beat butter, cream cheese, extra sugar and extract in a medium bowl with an electric mixer until pale and creamy. Beat in eggs, one at a time, until just combined. Add sifted flour, baking powder, nutmeg and salt; stir until just combined. Fold apple through cake mixture. Spoon mixture into pan.

4 Bake cake for 1 hour 35 minutes or until a skewer inserted into the centre comes out clean. Stand cake in pan for 15 minutes before turning, top-side down, onto a baking-paper-covered wire rack to cool.

5 Make brown butter frosting.

6 Spread frosting on cooled cake. Drizzle with reserved browned butter; dust with extra nutmeg.

BROWN BUTTER FROSTING Melt butter in a small frying pan over medium heat; cook for 2 minutes or until butter is nut brown. Cool slightly. Beat extra butter in a small bowl with an electric mixer until pale and creamy. Add sifted icing sugar, in three batches, beating until light and fluffy. Add extract and 2 tablespoons of the browned butter; beat until combined. Reserve remaining browned butter.

TIP It is best to pour the remaining brown butter over the cake just before serving or it will set. You can reheat the butter in a microwave on a low power setting if necessary.

DO-AHEAD Uniced cake can be made a day ahead; store in an airtight container at room temperature.

Poached quince
AND CHESTNUT CAKE

PREP + COOK TIME **4 HOURS** SERVES **12**

2 medium quince (700g), peeled, quartered, cored

2 cups (440g) caster (superfine) sugar

$^{1}/_{2}$ cup (125ml) sweet marsala

2 cinnamon sticks, halved

1 vanilla bean, split lengthways (see TECHNIQUES)

1 litre (4 cups) water

$1^{1}/_{4}$ cup (185g) self-raising flour

100g (3 ounces) ground almonds

$^{1}/_{2}$ teaspoon baking powder

1 teaspoon mixed spice

250g (8 ounces) butter, softened

1 cup (220g) firmly packed brown sugar

1 cup (220g) unsweetened chestnut puree

3 eggs

$^{1}/_{4}$ cup (60ml) milk

CRUMBLE TOPPING

$^{1}/_{3}$ cup (50g) plain (all-purpose) flour

$^{1}/_{3}$ cup (75g) firmly packed brown sugar

$^{2}/_{3}$ cup (80g) finely chopped walnuts

75g ($2^{1}/_{2}$ ounces) butter, chopped

1 Place quince, caster sugar, marsala, cinnamon, vanilla bean and the water in a large saucepan over high heat; bring to the boil. Reduce heat to low; simmer, uncovered, for 2 hours or until quince is tender and syrup has reduced. Using a slotted spoon, transfer quince into a medium bowl; cool. Reserve syrup and cinnamon. Discard vanilla bean. Cut quince quarters in half.

2 Meanwhile, make crumble topping.

3 Preheat oven to 180°C/350°F. Grease a deep 24cm ($9^{1}/_{2}$-inch) springform pan; line base with baking paper.

4 Push flour, ground almonds, baking powder and mixed spice through a fine sieve into a bowl. Beat butter and brown sugar in a large bowl with an electric mixer until paler and fluffy. Add chestnut puree; beat until smooth. Beat in eggs, one at a time, until just combined. Fold in flour mixture and milk until combined. Spread mixture into pan; arrange 12 quince wedges in a circular pattern, then place 4 wedges in the centre. Sprinkle crumble over quince.

5 Bake cake for $1^{1}/_{4}$ hours or until a skewer inserted into the centre comes out clean. Stand cake in pan for 10 minutes before transferring to a wire rack to cool. Serve warm or cooled, drizzled with reserved syrup and cinnamon.

CRUMBLE TOPPING Combine flour, sugar and walnuts in a small bowl. Rub in butter until mixture forms coarse crumbs.

TIP If syrup is a little thin, remove quince with a slotted spoon, then boil syrup, uncovered, for 5 minutes or until thicker.

TECHNIQUES Step 1: see also *'preparing vanilla beans'*, page 276.

DO-AHEAD The quince can be poached a day ahead; store in an airtight cake in the refrigerator. The cake is best made on day of serving.

Rhubarb, pear AND POMEGRANATE custard tea cakes

PREP + COOK TIME **1 HOUR** (+ COOLING) MAKES **8**

1 ripe small pear (180g), peeled, cored, sliced thinly
4 thin stalks rhubarb (250g), trimmed
1 medium pomegranate (320g)
100g (3 ounces) butter, softened
$1/_2$ cup (110g) caster (superfine) sugar
1 egg
$2/_3$ cup (100g) self-raising flour
2 tablespoons custard powder
2 tablespoons caster (superfine) sugar, extra

CINNAMON CUSTARD
1 tablespoon custard powder
$1/_4$ teaspoon ground cinnamon
2 tablespoons caster (superfine) sugar
$1/_2$ cup (125ml) milk
10g ($1/_2$ ounce) butter
$1/_2$ teaspoon vanilla extract

1 Make cinnamon custard.
2 Peel pear; core and thinly slice. Cut rhubarb lengthways into 1cm ($1/_2$-inch) wide long strips; cut strips into 7cm ($2^3/_4$-inch) lengths. Cut pomegranate in half crossways; hold one half over a bowl, tap the back with a wooden spoon to release seeds and juice. Strain seeds over a small jug; reserve seeds and juice separately. You need $1/_4$ cup (60ml) juice; make up any difference with water.
3 Preheat oven to 180°C/350°F. Grease an 8-hole ($3/_4$-cup/180ml) mini loaf pan; line base and long sides of each pan hole with a strip of baking paper.

4 Beat butter and sugar in a small bowl with an electric mixer until pale and fluffy. Beat in egg. Stir in sifted flour and custard powder. Spoon mixture into pan holes, spreading to cover the base; there will only be a small amount of mixture. Top with cinnamon custard (about 3 teaspoons per hole), spreading carefully over cake mixture. Alternate pear and rhubarb slices upright on top of custard; sprinkle with pomegranate seeds.
5 Bake cakes for 25 minutes or until a cake springs back when pressed lightly with finger.
6 Meanwhile, stir reserved pomegranate juice and extra sugar in a small saucepan over low heat until sugar dissolves. Bring to the boil; boil for 5 minutes or until thick and syrupy.
7 Stand cakes in pan for 5 minutes before lifting out onto plates. Brush top of warm cakes with warm syrup; serve cakes warm.

CINNAMON CUSTARD Blend custard powder, cinnamon and sugar with milk in a small saucepan; stir over medium heat until mixture boils and thickens. Cook, stirring, a further minute. Remove from heat; stir in butter and extract. Transfer to a small bowl; cover surface with plastic wrap. Cool.

TECHNIQUES Step 2: see *'removing seeds from a pomegranate'*, page 276.
DO-AHEAD The cakes are best made on day of serving.

Rhubarb and vanilla
CRUMBLE CAKE

PREP + COOK TIME 2 HOURS 20 MINUTES (+ COOLING & REFRIGERATION) SERVES 12

1 vanilla bean
700g (1½ pounds) trimmed rhubarb
½ cup (110g) caster (superfine) sugar
180g (5½ ounces) butter, softened
2 teaspoons vanilla extract
1⅓ cups (300g) caster (superfine) sugar, extra
3 eggs
¾ cup (180g) sour cream
1¼ cups (185g) self-raising flour
½ cup (75g) plain (all-purpose) flour
½ cup (40g) custard powder
2 teaspoons icing (confectioners') sugar

ALMOND CRUMBLE
¾ cup (110g) plain (all-purpose) flour
⅓ cup (75g) firmly packed brown sugar
80g (2½ ounces) butter, chopped
¼ cup (30g) natural sliced almonds]

1 Preheat oven to 180°C/350°F.
2 Split vanilla bean in half; scrape out seeds (see TECHNIQUES). Reserve seeds. Cut rhubarb into 2.5cm (1-inch) lengths; halve any thick stems lengthways. Combine rhubarb, caster sugar and vanilla bean in a shallow large ceramic ovenproof dish; spread rhubarb into a single layer. Roast for 25 minutes or until tender. Cool. Drain rhubarb; discard vanilla bean, reserve syrup.
3 Meanwhile, make almond crumble.

4 Grease a deep 23cm (9¼-inch) square cake pan; line base and sides with baking paper, extending the paper 5cm (2 inches) above edges.
5 Beat butter, reserved vanilla seeds, extract and extra caster sugar in a small bowl with an electric mixer until pale and fluffy. Beat in eggs, one at a time. Beat in sour cream. Transfer mixture to a large bowl. Stir in combined sifted flours and custard powder. Spread half the mixture into pan; top with half the rhubarb and half the almond crumble. Repeat layering.
6 Bake cake for 1 hour 20 minutes or until a skewer inserted into the centre comes out clean. Stand cake in pan for 5 minutes before turning, top-side up, onto a wire rack. Dust with sifted icing sugar. Serve cake warm with reserved rhubarb syrup.

ALMOND CRUMBLE Combine flour and sugar in a medium bowl; using your fingertips, rub in butter until mixture resembles coarse crumbs. Press mixture together with your fingers to create uneven lumps. Stir in almonds. Refrigerate for 20 minutes or until firm.

TIPS You will need about two bunches of rhubarb for this recipe. To spread the second layer of cake batter over the crumble, without mixing the two, dollop the batter into each corner first, then gently spread the batter toward the centre.
TECHNIQUES Step 2: see also *'preparing vanilla beans'*, page 276. Step 4: see *'lining a square cake pan'*, page 276.

Pure apple cake with golden syrup custard
[RECIPE PAGES 262 & 263]

Pure apple cake
WITH GOLDEN SYRUP CUSTARD

PREP + COOK TIME 3 HOURS (+ COOLING, REFRIGERATION & STANDING) SERVES 8

Made from little more than apples and a touch of spice, the long slow-cooking concentrates the apple taste. Serve as a dessert cake, perfect for guests with intolerances to wheat or gluten.

1 vanilla bean
1 cinnamon stick
2/3 cup (150g) caster (superfine) sugar
1/2 cup (125ml) apple juice
2 tablespoons lemon juice
80g (2 1/2 ounces) unsalted butter, chopped
10 large green apples (2kg)
2 teaspoons golden syrup, warmed

GOLDEN SYRUP CUSTARD
1 vanilla bean
1/2 cup (125ml) milk
1 cup (250ml) thickened (heavy) cream
1/4 cup (90g) golden syrup
4 egg yolks
2 tablespoons caster (superfine) sugar
1/2 cup (120g) mascarpone

1 Preheat oven to 180°C/350°F. Grease a 20cm (8-inch) springform pan; line base with baking paper. Place pan on a baking-paper-lined shallow oven tray.

2 Split vanilla bean in half; remove seeds (see TECHNIQUES). Place seeds and bean in a medium saucepan with cinnamon, sugar, juices and butter; stir over medium heat until sugar dissolves. Bring to the boil; simmer for 5 minutes until reduced slightly. Transfer to a large bowl.

3 Working with two apples at a time, peel and core eight of the apples; using a mandoline or sharp knife, cut apples into 3mm (1/8-inch) slices. Add sliced apple to syrup in bowl; toss to coat in syrup (this prevents the apple from discolouring). Drain apple slices from syrup. Arrange slices in springform pan, overlapping each slice by half. Cover the centre with smaller slices to create a tight fit. Press firmly on apples, twice during layering, pouring any excess liquid back into the saucepan.

4 Peel remaining apples, leaving stems intact. Using a mandoline, cut apples lengthways, including through core; remove seeds. Coat slices lightly in remaining syrup. Arrange overlapping slices in pan. Cover pan with baking paper, then with foil.

[PHOTOGRAPH PAGES 260 & 261]

5 Bake apple cake for 1 hour; remove foil and baking paper. Reduce oven to 140°C/280°F; bake a further 1 hour or until apple is soft and a knife can easily be inserted into the layers, brushing occasionally with some of the remaining cooking liquid. Cool to room temperature.

6 Cover surface of apple cake with baking paper; cover pan with plastic wrap. Refrigerate 4 hours or until cold and firm.

7 Meanwhile, make golden syrup custard.

8 To serve, run a knife around the apple cake and a hot cloth around the outside of the pan. Remove ring. Slide the base of a round tart pan under the cake; transfer it carefully onto a serving plate, removing the tart pan base as you place it on the plate. Stand cake at room temperature for 1 hour. Brush top with golden syrup; serve with golden syrup custard.

GOLDEN SYRUP CUSTARD Split vanilla bean in half; remove seeds (see TECHNIQUES). Add seeds and bean to a medium saucepan with milk and cream; stir over medium heat until almost boiling. Remove from heat; stir in syrup. Whisk egg yolks and sugar in a medium heatproof bowl; gradually whisk in hot milk mixture. Return to pan; stir over low heat for 3 minutes or until thick enough to coat the back of a spoon. Strain custard into a bowl; cover surface with plastic wrap. Cool. Whisk mascarpone in a medium bowl until smooth; gradually whisk in custard.

TIP It is best to use a serrated knife to cut this cake.
TECHNIQUES Steps 2 & 7: see also *'preparing vanilla beans'*, page 276.
DO-AHEAD The cake and custard can be made a day ahead; keep covered, in the refrigerator.

Pure apple cake
WITH GOLDEN SYRUP CUSTARD

[RECIPE PAGES 262 & 263]

SLICING THE APPLES
Slice the apples on a mandoline using the safety guard into 3mm (1/8-inch) slices. You could also use a sharp knife.

FLAVOURING THE APPLES SLICES
Toss the apple slices in the juice and butter mixture to prevent them browning and to add flavour.

LAYERING APPLE SLICES
Place the apple slices in the pan, overlapping them as you go, in layers as evenly as possible. Finish layering with the apple slices that have the stalks and core intact (ensure there are no seeds left in the core).

MAKING THE CUSTARD
Whisk the egg yolks and sugar together in a bowl. Gradually pour the cream mixture into the egg yolk mixture, whisking continuously until combined.

THICKENING THE CUSTARD
Return the combined mixture to the pan and stir over medium heat with a wooden spoon until mixture thickens sufficiently to coat the back of the spoon. To check, run your finger over the back of the spoon – a visible line should remain.

SERVING
Serve the apple cake, brushed with golden syrup and golden syrup custard. Cut the cake into slices using a serrated knife.

Poached pear, mascarpone AND DESSERT WINE CAKE

PREP + COOK TIME **50 MINUTES (+ COOLING & REFRIGERATION) SERVES 8**

You will need to make this recipe the day before.

6 medium beurre bosc pears (1.4kg)
1 vanilla bean
3½ cups (770g) caster (superfine) sugar
3 cups (750ml) sweet white wine
2 cups (500ml) water
500g (1 pound) mascarpone
¾ cup (180ml) thickened (heavy) cream
2 egg yolks
1 tablespoon icing (confectioners') sugar
60g (2 ounces) dark (semi-sweet) chocolate, grated
2 tablespoons brandy
375g (12 ounces) sponge finger biscuits

1 Peel pears, leaving stalks intact, then halve. Split vanilla bean in half lengthways; scrape seeds (see TECHNIQUES). Add seeds and bean to a large saucepan with sugar, wine and the water; stir over medium heat until sugar dissolves. Bring to the boil. Reduce heat; simmer for 1 minute. Add pears; cover pears with a round of baking paper and a small plate to keep pears submerged. Simmer for 15 minutes or until pears are tender. Cool.
2 Beat mascarpone, cream, egg yolks and icing sugar in a large bowl with an electric mixer until soft peaks form. Fold in grated chocolate. Cover; refrigerate until needed.
3 Line a 7.5cm (3-inch) deep, 10cm x 23cm (4-inch x 9¼-inch) loaf pan with plastic wrap, extending wrap over the sides.

4 Cut 2 pears into 1cm (½-inch) slices. Combine 2 cups (500ml) of the pear poaching liquid with brandy in a large bowl. Dip both sides of 8 or 9 biscuits, one at a time, into poaching liquid; place biscuits crossways into base of pan, trimming to fit if necessary. Spread 1½ cups (375ml) mascarpone mixture over biscuits; top with sliced pears, overlapping slightly. Spread a 5mm (¼-inch) layer of mascarpone mixture over pear layer. Dip 10 biscuits into poaching liquid; place lengthways on mascarpone layer, trimming to fit if necessary (changing the direction helps the biscuits fit into a loaf pan with slopping sides). Spread remaining mascarpone mixture over biscuits; finish layering with another 10 dipped biscuits. Tap pan lightly onto work surface to settle mixture. Cover with plastic wrap; refrigerate overnight.
5 Meanwhile, simmer 1 cup (250ml) of the poaching liquid and the vanilla bean in a small saucepan over medium heat for 5 minutes or until thickened. Cool; refrigerate until needed.
6 To serve, turn cake out of pan onto a platter; remove plastic wrap. Place half the pears and vanilla bean on top of cake; drizzle with thickened syrup. Serve cake with remaining pears.

TIPS We used moscato, a low alcohol, lightly sparkling Italian wine. We used a loaf pan with a capacity of 2.2 litres (9 cups). To line the pan smoothly with plastic wrap, dampen it first. When serving, you could cut the pears into quarters if you prefer.
TECHNIQUES Step 1: see also *'preparing vanilla beans'*, page 276.
DO-AHEAD This recipe needs to be prepared a day ahead. Decorate close to serving.

Quince brioche cake
[RECIPE PAGES 270 & 271]

Quince brioche cake

PREP + COOK TIME **6 HOURS (+ COOLING, REFRIGERATION & STANDING)** SERVES **8**

You will need to start this recipe the day before.

5 medium quinces (1.75kg)
$4^1/_2$ cups (990g) caster (superfine) sugar
3 cups (750ml) water
2 cups (500ml) rosé wine
8 black peppercorns
3 fresh bay leaves
2 vanilla beans, split lengthways (see TECHNIQUES)
1 teaspoon icing (confectioners') sugar

BRIOCHE
2 teaspoons (7g) dried yeast
$^1/_4$ cup (55g) caster (superfine) sugar
$^2/_3$ cup (160ml) lukewarm milk
4 egg yolks
2 cups (300g) '00' flour, bread flour or plain (all-purpose) flour
2 teaspoons sea salt flakes
80g ($2^1/_2$ ounces) butter, softened, chopped

ALMOND FRANGIPANE
80g ($2^1/_2$ ounces) butter, softened, chopped
$^1/_2$ cup (110g) caster (superfine) sugar
1 egg
1 cup (120g) ground almonds
1 tablespoon plain (all-purpose) flour

1 Preheat oven to 150°C/350°F.

2 Peel quince, reserve half the peel. Quarter quince, do not core.

3 Stir sugar, the water, wine, peppercorns, bay leaves and vanilla beans in a large cast iron casserole or baking dish over medium heat until sugar dissolves. Add quince and reserved peel, bring to the boil; cover with a piece of baking paper then cover tightly with foil, or a lid. (Make sure quince is submerged in the liquid.) Bake in oven 5 hours, turning twice, or until quince are tender and deep red in colour. Cool in syrup. Cover; refrigerate overnight.

4 Meanwhile, make brioche.

5 The next day, remove quince from syrup with a slotted spoon. Cut cores from quince; cut each quarter in half lengthways. Strain syrup; reserve bay leaves and vanilla bean, discard peel and peppercorns. Reserve 2 cups (500ml) of the syrup. Return quince to remaining syrup; stand until required. Place reserved syrup in a medium saucepan over medium heat; simmer for 5 minutes or until thickened. Cool.

6 Meanwhile, make almond frangipane.

7 Preheat oven 210°C/420°F.

8 Roll chilled brioche out on a well-floured sheet of baking paper into a 18cm x 34cm ($7^1/_4$-inch x $13^3/_4$-inch) oval shape. Lift paper with brioche onto a large oven tray. Spread frangipane on dough, leaving a 1.5cm ($^3/_4$-inch) border. Top with three-quarters of the quince, cover loosely with plastic wrap; set aside in a warm place for 20 minutes or until slightly risen.

9 Bake brioche for 25 minutes or until risen and browned, and dough is cooked through. Cool for 5 minutes. Serve brioche topped with remaining quince, reserved bay leaves and vanilla bean; drizzle with a little reduced syrup.

BRIOCHE Combine yeast, 1 tablespoon of the sugar and milk in a small bowl. Cover; stand in a warm place for 10 minutes or until frothy. Stir in yolks. Combine flour, salt and remaining sugar in a large bowl of an electric mixer fitted with a dough hook. Add yeast mixture, mix on low speed until combined. Mix on medium speed for 5 minutes or until dough is smooth and elastic. Add butter, a small piece at a time, mixing until smooth. Transfer dough to a large oiled bowl, cover tightly with three layers of plastic wrap; refrigerate at least 4 hours or overnight. (To make brioche without an electric mixer, combine ingredients in a bowl using a wooden spoon, turn out onto a well-floured work surface and knead for 5 minutes or until smooth. Mixture will be sticky. Add butter a piece at a time, kneading each piece in well before adding the next until smooth.)

ALMOND FRANGIPANE Beat butter and sugar in a small bowl with an electric mixer until creamy. Beat in egg. Stir in ground almonds and flour.

TIPS We poached the quince in a syrup based on rosé wine, however you could use a light red or white wine if you prefer. For a non-alcoholic syrup use verjuice (the juice of unripe grapes). For a quick custard to serve with the brioche, stir 2 tablespoons of the reduced syrup into ready-made thick custard.
TECHNIQUES Step 3: see also *'preparing vanilla beans'*, page 276.
DO-AHEAD You will need to make the brioche and quince a day ahead as they both need to be refrigerated overnight. The almond frangipane can also be made a day ahead, however you will need to bring it back to room temperature before use in order for it to be spreadable.

[PHOTOGRAPH PAGES 268 & 269]

APPLE TYPES

The best cooking apple for a cake is one that holds its shape, isn't too wet and has a balanced sweet/tart flavour. In general green varieties such as golden delicious and granny smith are better, though red types such as pink lady and royal gala can be used for some recipes.

Measuring cups

IF USING MEASURING CUPS, ENSURE THAT YOU FILL AND LEVEL INGREDIENTS, AND WHERE AN INGREDIENT IS SPECIFIED 'FIRMLY PACKED', SUCH AS BROWN SUGAR, PRESS IT INTO THE CUP. FOR INGREDIENTS LIKE FLOUR, ALWAYS MEASURE FIRST BEFORE SIFTING.

QUINCE MAGIC *Is a large, yellow-skinned knobbly fruit that appears on grocers' shelves during the winter months. The perfumed flesh is inedible raw and, like apples and pears, it is prone to browning. Cooked slowly with sugar the flesh is transformed into a jewel-like red colour and aromatic taste.*

Heavy-based SAUCEPANS

For recipes such as custards and caramels use a pan with a heavy base. Both milk and caramel contain sugar so a thin cooking base will cause hot spots where the milk or caramel will scald.

WHAT GOES WITH APPLES & PEARS

Apples and pears are autumn fruits that partner well with the warm flavours of spice, roasted nuts, fortified wines, woody herbs and dark sugars. However they can also be presented in a light way with floral dessert wines and citrus.

RUBY COLOURED QUINCE

If you want to guarantee that your quince turn the quintessential deep-red colour, you can help the process along by replacing one-third of the cooking water with red wine.

Quince varieties

Quinces are never identified by variety when sold, though it's useful to know that there are differences between them. For example, some cook to a mid-pink tone, others more of a rusty red and others a deep garnet. Cooking times can also be shorter or longer between types.

TO PREVENT BROWNING To prevent quince, pears and apples browning, brush them with a little lemon juice. For cakes, avoid putting them into water with lemon juice, as the extra moisture might affect the cake.

PICKING PEARS

Unlike apples which are picked ripe, pears are picked hard and best ripened at room temperature; which takes between 3-8 days. To accelerate ripening, place pears with ethylene producing fruits such as bananas and apples, either in a paper bag or beside them in a fruit bowl. To check for ripeness, press gently at the neck end; the fruit will give a little if it's ripe; once ripened eat or refrigerate as the fruit will deteriorate very quickly.

COOKING PEARS

THE MOST ROBUST PEAR FOR COOKING IS THE LONG-NECKED BROWN-SKINNED BUERRE BOSC, WHICH SUITS ROASTING, POACHING, SAUTEEING AND BAKING. THE SMALLER GREENISH/RED CORELLA IS ANOTHER CHOICE FOR POACHING.

Maple syrup and persimmon
UPSIDE-DOWN CAKE

PREP + COOK TIME 2 HOURS 15 MINUTES (+ COOLING) SERVES 12

1 cup (250ml) maple syrup
220g (7 ounces) unsalted butter, softened, chopped
3 persimmons (fuji) (600g), sliced thinly
1 1/2 cups (330g) caster (superfine) sugar
1 tablespoon finely grated lemon rind
3 eggs, separated
1 1/2 teaspoons vanilla extract
3/4 cup (115g) plain (all-purpose) flour
1 1/2 teaspoons baking powder
3/4 cup (180ml) milk
1 1/2 cups (270g) fine semolina
3/4 cup (100g) coarsely chopped pistachios
2 persimmons (fuji) (400g), extra, sliced

1 Preheat oven to 170°C/340°F. Grease a 24cm (9 1/2-inch) round cake pan; line base with baking paper.

2 Stir maple syrup and 75g (2 1/2 ounces) of the butter in a small saucepan over low heat for 2 minutes or until butter melts. Increase heat to medium; bring to the boil. Boil for 4 minutes or until mixture thickens. Cool for 5 minutes.

3 Pour half the maple syrup mixture over base of cake pan (reserve remaining mixture in saucepan); arrange persimmon slices on base, positioning them slightly up the side of the pan.

4 Beat remaining butter with sugar and rind in a medium bowl with an electric mixer for 6 minutes or until pale and fluffy. Beat in egg yolks and extract until combined. Add combined sifted flour and baking powder, and milk; beat on low speed until almost combined. Add semolina; beat until combined.

5 Beat egg whites in another medium bowl with electric mixer until firm peaks form; gently fold into cake mixture. Carefully spread mixture evenly over persimmon; scatter with nuts.

6 Bake cake for 1 hour 20 minutes or until a skewer inserted into the centre comes out clean. Stand cake in pan for 30 minutes. Run a palette knife around the edge of the cake, then turn out onto a serving plate.

7 Add extra persimmon to reserved syrup mixture. Place pan over low heat; cook, turning slices for 5 mintues or until well coated. Top cake with persimmon and syrup mixture.

TIP Persimmons are an autumn fruit of which there are two types − an astringent one, eaten soft and a non-astringent firm variety, also known as fuji fruit. We've used the non-astringent variety in this recipe.

TECHNIQUES Step 1: see *'lining a round cake pan'*, page 276.

DO-AHEAD This cake is best made on day of serving.

LINING A ROUND CAKE PAN
Cut a strip of baking paper
wide enough to cover the side
of the pan extending below
and above the side; make a
2cm-fold along one edge, snip
at intervals. Cut a round of
paper using pan as a guide.
Grease pan; place strip around
side and round on base.

LINING A SQUARE CAKE PAN
Cut strips of baking paper
long enough to cover the
base and sides of the pan,
extending over the sides.
Grease base and sides of pan,
positioning paper in opposite
directions; grease between
strips to keep them in place.
Smooth out the surfaces.

**COOKING FILLO SO IT
STAYS FLAT** Place the fillo
rectangles on lined trays;
stack trays on top of one
another, so each layer of fillo
is weighted by the tray above.
The trays either need to be
very flat or slightly smaller
than one another to sit inside
each other.

MAKING DULCE DE LECHE
Place condensed milk in the
specified dish. Cover with
foil, scrunching it upwards
to ensure it doesn't touch
the water. Place in a larger
ovenproof dish; fill with
boiling water to come half
way up side of smaller dish.
Cook as directed in the recipe.

PREPARING VANILLA BEANS
Split the vanilla bean in half
lengthways using a sharp
knife. Holding the end of one
half, scrape the seeds out
from each half using the tip
of the knife.

**REMOVING SEEDS FROM
A POMEGRANATE** Using a
knife, cut pomegranate in
half crossways. Hold a half,
cut-side down over a bowl;
hit all over the outside with a
wooden spoon, to release the
seeds. Discard any white pith.

SEGMENTING CITRUS Cut
top and bottom off the fruit.
Following the curve of the
fruit, cut away the skin with
the white pith. Holding the
fruit over a bowl, cut down
either side of each segment
between the membrane to
release the segment.

**CUTTING PINEAPPLE (for
Upside-down pineapple and
ginger sour cream cake p178)**
Trim top and bottom from
pineapple; cut off the skin.
Cut into quarters lengthways;
remove cores. Cut quarters
crossways into 12 thin slices.
You will have 48 slices.

DISSOLVING GELATINE SHEETS Fill a wide medium bowl with cold water. Place gelatine sheets, one after the other, into the water; soak for 3 minutes or until soft and pliable. Gather up gelatine; squeeze out excess water. Use as directed.

DISSOLVING POWDERED GELATINE Sprinkle gelatine over water (or other liquid) in a small heatproof jug. Fill a small frying pan with enough water to reach the same level as the gelatine mixture in the jug; bring to a gentle simmer. Place jug in simmering water; stir until gelatine dissolves.

MAKING CARAMEL AND PRALINE Stir sugar and the water over medium heat without boiling, until sugar dissolves. Brush any crystals on the side of the pan with a wet pastry brush. Boil, without stirring, until golden. For praline, pour over nuts on a baking-paper-lined oven tray.

CUTTING CINNAMON, APPLE AND PECAN PULL-APART Using a sharp knife, cut eight equally spaced slits into the outside of the ring, towards the centre, cutting three quarters of the way in but not all the way through to the other side.

MELTING CHOCOLATE Bring a small saucepan filled with one-third of water to a simmer. Place chocolate in a small heatproof bowl on the pan, ensuring the bowl doesn't touch the water. Stir until melted and smooth; remove bowl immediately.

LEVELLING A CAKE Using a large finely serrated knife, hold the knife flat at the level you want to trim the cake. Keeping the knife flat, cut through the cake as evenly as possible. Discard trimmings.

SPLITTING A CAKE INTO EVEN LAYERS Use a ruler to measure out even layers; cut shallow slits at equal intervals around the cake. If cutting into three layers, start with the top layer first. Cut layers using the slits as a guide. Lift away cut layer with a wide spatula or a tart pan base.

DECORATING CAKES WITHOUT MAKING A MESS Place cake on a stand. Tuck strips of baking paper just under the cake to collect drips and smudges. Decorate as instructed. Ease away paper strips, one at a time, leaving the stand clean.

TYPES

There are many brands of cake pans on the market made from differing materials. We prefer pans made from aluminium as it is a great conductor of heat, produces an even golden crust, and for sponges in particular is hard to beat. Pans with non-stick coatings, or that are anodised or made from stainless or tin tend to accelerate cooking times, best results are obtained by reducing the oven temperature by 10°C or 25°F. Non-stick and anodised pans are useful for bundt shaped pans or other intricately shaped pans where batter can potentially stick. We always measure cake pans from the inside top measurement. Take care in particular with springform pans as strangely the size listed on the pan does not always correspond to the pan's closed size.

USING NEW CAKE PANS

Ovens do vary, so when you use a new cake pan for the first time, it's always a good idea to make a note of the oven temperature and baking time on the recipe for future reference.

Substituting PANS

To substitute one cake pan for another, find the pan listed in the recipe in the chart below, note what the litre/cup capacity is, then find another shaped pan with either the same, or very similar capacity. Keep in mind that if the recipe called for a springform pan and you swap it to a solid-based pan that the cake will need to be inverted to be removed. You will need to keep in mind that the cooking time may need to be adjusted in particular if you're swapping from a bundt pan to another shape.

DEEP ROUND CAKE PANS

15cm (6-inch) 1.125 litres (4$^1/_2$ cups)
20cm (8-inch) 2 litres (8 cups)
22cm (9-inch) 2.5 litres (10 cups)
24cm (9$^1/_2$-inch) 3.125 litres (12$^1/_2$ cups)
26cm (10$^1/_2$-inch) 3.5 litres (14 cups)

SPRINGFORM PANS

10cm (4-inch) 1 cup (250ml)
20cm (8-inch) 1.75 litres (7 cups)
21cm (8$^1/_2$-inch) 2 litres (8 cups)
22cm (9-inch) 2.125 litres (8$^1/_2$ cups)
23cm (9$^1/_4$-inch) 2.5 litres (10 cups)
24cm (9$^3/_4$-inch) 2.75 litres (11 cups)
26cm (10$^1/_2$-inch) 3.25 litres (13 cups)

SPECIAL CAKE PANS

11cm (4$^1/_2$-inch) kugelhopf 1 cup (250ml)
18cm (7$^1/_4$-inch) heart 1.25 litres (5 cups)
deep 21cm (8$^1/_2$-inch) bundt
  2.25 litres (9 cups)
21cm (8$^1/_2$-inch) kugelhopf
  2.25 litres (9 cups)
deep (10cm/4-inch) 22cm (9-inch) tube
  3 litres (12 cups)
22cm (9-inch) bundt 1.75 litres (7 cups)
24cm (9$^1/_2$-inch) bundt 2.75 litres (11 cups)
angel food cake pan There is no substitute.
swiss roll pans If your pan is slightly longer in one direction but not both it is okay to use.

MULTI-HOLED PANS

friand pans $^1/_3$ cup (80ml)
12-hole muffin pans $^1/_3$ cup (80ml)
6-hole texas muffin pans $^3/_4$ cup (180ml)
mini loaf pans $^3/_4$ cup (180ml)

LOAF PANS

10cm x 25cm x 7.5cm (4-inch x 10-inch x 3-inch) 1.5 litres (6 cups)
15cm x 23.5cm x 9cm (6-inch x 9$^1/_2$-inch x 3$^3/_4$-inch) 2.5 litres (9 cups)

SQUARE CAKE PANS

19cm (7$^3/_4$-inch) 2.5 litres (10 cups)
20cm (8-inch) 3 litres (12 cups)
22cm (9-inch) and 23cm (9$^1/_4$-inch) both sizes 3.75 litres (15 cups)

There is good reason for a recipe to state whether a cake pan has to be greased, greased and lined, or greased and floured. Follow recipes as directed.

ALLSPICE so-named because it tastes like a combination of nutmeg, cumin, clove and cinnamon. Available whole or ground.

ALMONDS flat, pointy-tipped nuts with a pitted brown shell enclosing a creamy white kernel which is covered by a brown skin.

flaked paper-thin slices.

ground also known as almond meal.

slivered small pieces cut lengthways

BAKING PAPER also called parchment or baking parchment; a silicone-coated paper used primarily for lining baking pans and oven trays so cakes and biscuits won't stick, making removal easy.

BAKING POWDER a raising agent consisting mainly of two parts cream of tartar to one part bicarbonate of soda (baking soda).

BAY LEAVES aromatic leaves from the bay tree; adds a strong, slightly peppery flavour.

BEETROOT (BEETS) also known as red beets; firm, round root vegetable.

BICARBONATE OF SODA (BAKING SODA) a raising agent.

BUTTER we use salted butter unless stated otherwise; 125g is equal to 1 stick (4 ounces).

unsalted simply has no salt added. It is mainly used in baking; if a recipe calls for unsalted butter, then it should be used.

CARDAMOM a spice native to india and used extensively in its cuisine; can be purchased in pod, seed or ground form. Has a distinctive aromatic, sweetly rich flavour.

CHEESE

cream commonly called philadelphia or philly; a soft cow-milk cheese, its fat content ranges from 14% to 33%.

mascarpone an Italian fresh cultured-cream product made similarly to yoghurt. Whiteish to creamy yellow in colour, with a buttery-rich, luscious texture. Soft, creamy and spreadable, it is used in Italian desserts.

ricotta a soft, sweet, moist, white cow-milk cheese with a low fat content and a slightly grainy texture.

CHESTNUT PUREE found in specialist food stores, delicatessens and some supermarkets.

CHOCOLATE

couverture a term used to describe a fine quality, very rich chocolate high in both cocoa butter and cocoa liquor. This type of chocolate requires tempering when used to coat but not if it is used in baking, mousses or fillings.

dark (semi-sweet) also called luxury chocolate; made of a high percentage of cocoa liquor and cocoa butter, and little added sugar.

milk mild and very sweet; similar in make-up to dark chocolate, the difference being the addition of milk solids.

white contains no cocoa solids but is a mixture of cocoa butter, milk solids and sugar. It is very sensitive to heat.

CINNAMON available in pieces (called sticks or quills) and ground into powder; one of the world's most common spices, used as a sweet, fragrant flavouring for both sweet and savoury foods.

CLOVES dried flower buds of a tropical tree; can be used whole or in ground form. They have a strong scent and taste so should be used sparingly.

COCOA POWDER also called cocoa; dried, unsweetened, roasted and ground cocoa beans (cacao seeds).

dutch-processed is treated with an alkali to neutralise its acids. It has a reddish-brown colour, a mild flavour and is easy to dissolve.

COCONUT

cream obtained commercially from the first pressing of the coconut flesh alone, without the addition of water; the second pressing (less rich) is sold as coconut milk. Available in cans and cartons at most supermarkets.

desiccated concentrated, dried, unsweetened and finely shredded coconut flesh.

flaked dried flaked coconut flesh.

shredded unsweetened thin strips of dried coconut flesh.

CORNFLOUR (CORNSTARCH) used as a thickening agent. Available as 100% maize (corn) and wheaten cornflour.

CREAM

pouring also called pure or fresh cream. It contains no additives and has a minimum fat content of 35%.

sour a thick, commercially-cultured sour cream with a minimum fat content of 35%.

thick (double) a dolloping cream with a minimum fat content of 45%.

thickened (heavy) a whipping cream that contains a thickener. It has a minimum fat content of 35%.

CREAM OF TARTAR the acid ingredient in baking powder; added to confectionery mixtures to help prevent sugar from crystallising. Keeps frostings creamy and improves volume when beating egg whites.

CRÈME FRAÎCHE a mature, naturally fermented cream (minimum fat content 35%) with a velvety texture and slightly tangy, nutty flavour. It can boil without curdling.

FILLO PASTRY paper-thin sheets of raw pastry. Brush each sheet with oil or melted butter, stack in layers; cut and fold as directed.

FLOUR

baker's also known as gluten-enriched, strong or bread-mix flour. Produced from a variety of what has a high gluten (protein) content and is best suited for pizza and bread making: the expansion caused by the yeast and the stretchiness imposed by kneading require a flour that is "strong" enough to handle these stresses.

plain (all-purpose) unbleached wheat flour, is the best for baking: the gluten content ensures a strong dough, for a light result.

rice very fine, almost powdery, gluten-free flour; made from ground white rice. Used in baking, as a thickener, and in some Asian noodles and desserts.

self-raising all-purpose plain or wholemeal flour with baking powder and salt added; make at home in the proportion of 1 cup flour to 2 teaspoons baking powder.

FOOD COLOURING vegetable-based substance available in liquid, paste or gel form. Available from supermarkets.

GELATINE a thickening agent; available dried (powdered) gelatine and in sheets (leaf) gelatine. Three teaspoons of dried gelatine (8g or one sachet) equals about four leaves. For titanium-strength gelatine, it is more accurate to follow the weight directed in the recipe rather than the number of sheets.

GINGER

fresh also called green or root ginger; the thick gnarled root of a tropical plant.

glacé fresh ginger root preserved in sugar syrup; crystallised ginger (sweetened with cane sugar) can be substituted if rinsed with warm water and dried before using.

ground also called powdered ginger; used as a flavouring in baking but cannot be substituted for fresh ginger.

GLUCOSE SYRUP also known as liquid glucose, made from wheat starch; used in jam and confectionery making. Available at health-food stores and supermarkets.

GOLDEN SYRUP a by-product of refined sugarcane; pure maple syrup or honey can be substituted. Treacle is more viscous, and has a stronger flavour and aroma than golden syrup.

GREASING/OILING PANS use butter or margarine for sweet baking; use cooking-oil spray or oil, for savoury baking. Overgreasing pans can cause food to overbrown. Use paper towel or a pastry brush to spread the oil or butter over the pan.

HAZELNUTS also known as filberts; plump, grape-sized, rich, sweet nut having a brown skin that is removed by rubbing heated nuts together vigorously in a tea-towel.

ground is made by grinding the hazelnuts to a coarse flour texture for use in baking or as a thickening agent.

HONEY the variety sold in a squeezable container is not suitable for the recipes in this book.

KAFFIR LIME LEAVES also called bai magrood, sold fresh, dried or frozen; looks like two glossy dark green leaves joined end to end, forming a rounded hourglass shape.

Dried leaves are less potent, so double the number called for in a recipe if you substitute them for fresh. A strip of fresh lime peel may be substituted for each kaffir lime leaf.

LEMON GRASS a tall, clumping, lemon-smelling and -tasting, sharp-edged grass; the white lower part of the stem is chopped and used cooking. Bruise the lower white bulb with the flat side of a heavy knife to release the flavour and aroma.

LIQUEUR

cherry-flavoured such as kirsch

chocolate-flavoured such as crème de cacao.

coffee-flavoured such as kahlua or tia maria.

hazelnut-flavoured such as frangelico.

limoncello Italian lemon-flavoured liqueur; originally made from the juice and peel of lemons grown along the Amalfi coast.

orange-flavoured such as curaçao, grand marnier or cointreau.

MAPLE-FLAVOURED SYRUP is made from sugar cane and is also called golden or pancake syrup. It is not a substitute for pure maple syrup.

MAPLE SYRUP, PURE distilled from the sap of sugar maple trees found only in Canada and the USA. Maple-flavoured syrup or pancake syrup is not an adequate substitute for the real thing.

MARSALA a fortified Italian wine produced in the region surrounding the Sicilian city of Marsala; has an intense amber colour and complex aroma. We used the sweet variety.

MILK

caramel top 'n' fill a canned milk product consisting of condensed milk that has been boiled to a caramel.

sweetened condensed a canned milk product consisting of milk with more than half the water content removed and sugar added to the remaining milk.

MIXED SPICE a classic spice mixture generally containing caraway, allspice, coriander, cumin, nutmeg and ginger, although cinnamon and other spices can be added. It is used with fruit and in cakes.

MOLASSES a thick, dark brown syrup, the residue from the refining of sugar; available in light, dark and blackstrap varieties.

MUSCAT a sweet, fruity dessert wine, made from the grape of the same name. Is almost caramel in colour.

MUSCATELS, DRIED made by drying large muscatel grapes (grown exclusively around Malagna in Spain). They are partially dried in the sun, then drying is completed indoors; they are left on the stalk and pressed flat for sale. Muscatel is a sweet wine made from the grapes.

MUSLIN a loosely-woven cotton fabric used to separate liquid from solids. You could also use a clean Chux cloth.

NUTMEG a strong and pungent spice ground from the dried nut of an evergreen tree native to indonesia. Usually found ground but the flavour is more intense from a whole nut, available from spice shops, so it's best to grate your own.

OIL

cooking spray we use a cholesterol-free cooking spray made from canola oil.

olive made from ripened olives. Extra virgin and virgin are the first and second press, respectively, of the olives and are therefore considered the best; "light" refers to taste not fat levels.

vegetable oils sourced from plant rather than animal fats.

ORANGE FLOWER WATER concentrated flavouring made from orange blossoms. Available from Middle-Eastern food stores and some delicatessens. Cannot be substituted with cirtus flavourings, as the taste is completely different.

PEANUTS not in fact a nut but the pod of a legume. We mainly use raw (unroasted) or unsalted roasted peanuts.

PERSIMMONS there are two types available: astringent and non-astringent. Astringent persimmons are heart shaped and eaten very ripe, otherwise the taste is very astringent. Non-astringent persimmons, sometimes sold as fuji fruit (Japanese for persimmon), are squat shaped and eaten crisp.

PINE NUTS also called pignoli; not a nut but a small, cream-coloured kernel from pine cones. They are best roasted before use to bring out the flavour.

PISTACHIOS green, delicately flavoured nuts inside hard off-white shells. Available unshelled or shelled and unsalted or salted from supermarkets and health food stores.

POACHING a cooking term to describe gentle simmering of food in liquid; spices or herbs can be added to impart their flavour.

POLENTA also known as cornmeal; a flour-like cereal made of dried corn (maize).

POMEGRANATE dark-red, leathery-skinned fresh fruit about the size of an orange filled with hundreds of seeds, each wrapped in an edible lucent-crimson pulp having a unique tangy sweet-sour flavour.

POPPY SEEDS small, dried, bluish-grey seeds of the poppy plant, with a crunchy texture and a nutty flavour. Can be purchased whole or ground in delicatessens and most supermarkets.

QUINCE yellow-skinned fruit with hard texture and astringent, tart taste; eaten cooked or as a preserve. Long, slow cooking makes the flesh a deep rose pink.

RHUBARB a plant with long, green-red stalks; becomes sweet and edible when cooked.

ROASTING/TOASTING nuts and dried coconut can be roasted in the oven to restore their fresh flavour and release their aromatic essential oils. Spread them evenly onto an oven tray; roast in a 180°C/350°F oven for about 5 minutes. Desiccated coconut, pine nuts and sesame seeds roast more evenly if stirred over low heat in a heavy-based frying pan; their natural oils will help turn them golden brown.

ROSEWATER extract made from crushed rose petals, called gulab in india; used for its aromatic quality in many sweetmeats and desserts.

SEGMENTING a cooking term to describe cutting citrus fruits in such a way that pieces contain no pith, seed or membrane. The peeled fruit is cut towards the centre inside each membrane, forming wedges. See also *'segmenting citrus'*, page 276.

SEMOLINA coarsely ground flour milled from durum wheat; the flour used in making gnocchi, pasta and couscous.

SESAME SEEDS black and white are the most common of this small oval seed. Roast the seeds in a heavy-based frying pan over low heat.

SHERRY fortified wine consumed as an aperitif or used in cooking. Sherries differ in colour and flavour; sold as fino (light, dry), amontillado (medium sweet, dark) and oloroso (full-bodied, very dark).

SPONGE FINGER BISCUITS also known as savoiardi, savoy biscuits or lady's fingers, they are Italian-style crisp fingers made from sponge cake mixture.

STAR ANISE dried star-shaped pod with an astringent aniseed flavour; used to flavour desserts, as well as stocks and marinades. Available whole and ground.

SUGAR

brown a very soft, finely granulated sugar retaining molasses for its characteristic colour and flavour.

caster (superfine) finely granulated table sugar; dissolves easily.

demerara small-grained golden-coloured crystal sugar.

icing (confectioners') also called powdered sugar; pulverised granulated sugar crushed together with a small amount of cornflour (cornstarch).

muscovado a fine-grained, moist sugar that comes in two types:, light and dark.

palm also called nam tan pip, jaggery, jawa or gula melaka; made from the sap of the sugar palm tree. Light brown to black in colour and usually sold in rock-hard cakes; use with brown sugar if unavailable.

pure icing (confectioners') also known as powdered sugar.

raw natural brown granulated sugar.

vanilla is available in supermarkets, usually among the spices. Or, you can make your own by putting a couple of vanilla beans in a jar of caster sugar.

white (granulated) coarse, granulated table sugar, also known as crystal sugar.

SULTANAS also called golden raisins; dried seedless white grapes.

SUMAC a purple-red, astringent spice ground from berries growing on shrubs that flourish wild around the mediterranean; adds a tart, lemony flavour to dips and dressings and goes well with barbecued meat. Can be found in Middle Eastern food stores.

TREACLE thick, dark syrup not unlike molasses; a by-product of sugar refining.

VANILLA

bean dried, long, thin pod from a tropical golden orchid; the minuscule black seeds inside the bean impart a luscious flavour in baking and desserts. (See also *'preparing vanilla beans'*, page 276.) Place a whole bean in a jar of sugar to make vanilla sugar; a bean can be used three or four times.

extract obtained from vanilla beans infused in water; a non-alcoholic version of essence.

paste made from vanilla beans and contains real seeds. Is highly concentrated: 1 teaspoon replaces a whole vanilla bean. Found in most supermarkets in the baking section.

VINEGAR, WHITE made from distilled grain alcohol.

YEAST (dried and fresh), a raising agent used in dough making. Granular (7g sachets) and fresh compressed (20g blocks) yeast can almost always be substituted for the other when yeast is called for.

YOGHURT we use plain full-cream yoghurt in our recipes.

Greek-style plain yoghurt strained in a cloth (traditionally muslin) to remove the whey and to give it a creamy consistency.

MEASURES

One Australian metric measuring cup holds approximately 250ml; one Australian metric tablespoon holds 20ml; one Australian metric teaspoon holds 5ml. The difference between one country's measuring cups and another's is within a two- or three-teaspoon variance, and will not affect your cooking results. North America, New Zealand and the United Kingdom use 15ml tablespoons. All cup and spoon measurements are level.

The most accurate way of measuring dry ingredients is to weigh them. When measuring liquids, use a clear glass or plastic jug with the metric markings. We use large eggs with an average weight of 60g.

OVEN TEMPERATURES

The oven temperatures in this book are for conventional ovens; if you have a fan-forced oven, decrease the temperature by 10-20 degrees.

	°C (CELSIUS)	°F (FAHRENHEIT)
Very slow	120	250
Slow	150	300
Moderately slow	160	325
Moderate	180	350
Moderately hot	200	400
Hot	220	425
Very hot	240	475

DRY MEASURES

METRIC	IMPERIAL
15g	$^1/_2$oz
30g	1oz
60g	2oz
90g	3oz
125g	4oz ($^1/_4$ lb)
155g	5oz
185g	6oz
220g	7oz
250g	8oz ($^1/_2$ lb)
280g	9oz
315g	10oz
345g	11oz
375g	12oz ($^3/_4$ lb)
410g	13oz
440g	14oz
470g	15oz
500g	16oz (1lb)
750g	24oz (1$^1/_2$ lb)
1kg	32oz (2lb)

LIQUID MEASURES

METRIC	IMPERIAL
30ml	1 fluid oz
60ml	2 fluid oz
100ml	3 fluid oz
125ml	4 fluid oz
150ml	5 fluid oz
190ml	6 fluid oz
250ml	8 fluid oz
300ml	10 fluid oz
500ml	16 fluid oz
600ml	20 fluid oz
1000ml	1$^3/_4$ pints

LENGTH MEASURES

METRIC	IMPERIAL
3mm	$^1/_8$in
6mm	$^1/_4$in
1cm	$^1/_2$in
2cm	$^3/_4$in
2.5cm	1in
5cm	2in
6cm	2$^1/_2$in
8cm	3in
10cm	4in
13cm	5in
15cm	6in
18cm	7in
20cm	8in
23cm	9in
25cm	10in
28cm	11in
30cm	12in (1ft)

FIRST PUBLISHED IN 2014
BY OCTOPUS PUBLISHING GROUP LIMITED BASED ON MATERIALS
LICENSED TO IT BY BAUER MEDIA BOOKS, AUSTRALIA
THIS EDITION REPRINTED IN 2015
BAUER MEDIA BOOKS IS A DIVISION OF BAUER MEDIA PTY LIMITED
54 PARK ST, SYDNEY; GPO BOX 4088, SYDNEY, NSW 2001, AUSTRALIA
PHONE (+61) 2 9282 8618; FAX (+61) 2 9126 3702
WWW.AWWCOOKBOOKS.COM.AU

BAUER
MEDIA GROUP

BAUER MEDIA BOOKS

Publisher Jo Runciman
Editorial & food director Pamela Clark
Director of sales, marketing & rights Brian Cearnes
Art director & designer Hannah Blackmore
Senior editor Stephanie Kistner
Food concept director & food editor Sophia Young

PUBLISHED BY

Published and Distributed in the United Kingdom by Octopus Publishing Group
Carmelite House
50 Victoria Embankment
London, EC4Y 0DZ
United Kingdom
info@octopus-publishing.co.uk; www.octopusbooks.co.uk

Printed by C&C Offset Printing, China.

International foreign language rights
Brian Cearnes, Bauer Media Books bcearnes@bauer-media.com.au

A catalogue record for this book is available from the British Library.

ISBN: 978-1-74245-475-7 (hardback)

© Bauer Media Pty Limited 2014

ABN 18 053 273 546